Brainteasers for the BBC and Electron computers

Brainteasers
for the
BBC and Electron computers

Geneviève Ludinski

Phoenix Publishing Associates
Bushey, Herts.

Copyright © Geneviève Ludinski
All rights reserved

First published in Great Britain by
PHOENIX PUBLISHING ASSOCIATES
14 Vernon Road, Bushey, Herts. WD2 2JL

ISBN 0 9465 7603 3

Printed in Great Britain by
Billing & Sons Limited
Cover design by
David Berkoff
Typesetting by
Prestige Press (UK) Ltd.

CONTENTS

Introduction	1
Hexagon Puzzle	2
Safecracker	6
Fractions and Percentages	10
A-Maze-Ing	14
Saints to Sinners	18
Spot the Difference	23
Relations	28
Don't Paint the Cat	33
Francis Drake Adventure Game	37
Name the Graph	47
Close Encounters of the Fourth Kind	51
Sequence Countdown	55
Spiral Mazes	59
What's Yours	62
Pattern Pairs	66
Concentration Test	70
Wire Maze	74
Profit and Loss	78
Odd One Out	83
Decisive Hero	86
Fraction Car Chase	91
Western Adventure Game	95
Detective	99
Elementary Statistics	104
3-D Brainstorm	109
Bar Charter	114
Stats Painter	118
Who Dunnit	122
Word Search	126

INTRODUCTION

Before you dive into this book, here are a few tips you may find useful when keying in the programs.

You may miss out all the REM statements except the first two. These statements are just to help you understand how the program works.

You can also omit the spaces between the line number and the start of the statement. However BBC BASIC is rather pedantic about spaces elsewhere, so I advise you to copy the rest of the statement exactly. In particular, there may be no spaces between TAB and the first bracket. Also, to be safe, always put a space before words OR and AND. Any spaces within quotation marks must also be copied exactly.

Remember also to put in all the punctuation exactly as it appears. If you miss out a comma, the prgram may not work. If the program still does not work after you have corrected the errors reported by the computer, check the following. See whether you have confused any zeros for the letter O, or alternatively ones and the letter I. Check, also, that you have not missed any program lines. This is easily done if program lines look similar. Most program line numbers go up by ten at a time, so read your line numbers to find this one.

You may find some of the procedures useful, and you are welcome to put these in any programs you write for your own use. You may not, of course, sell or give them away.

I hope you enjoy the book, and that your brain is not teased too heavily.

HEXAGON PUZZLE

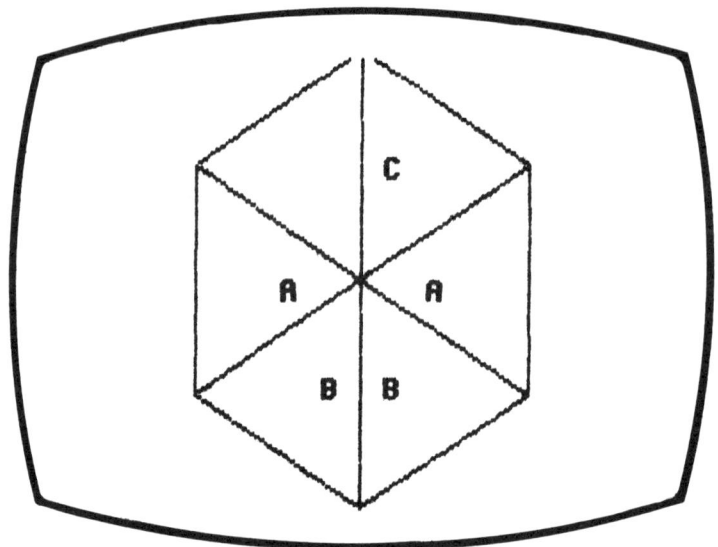

You are really up against the clock on this one as you must solve as many puzzles as possible, in just 200 seconds. A series of numbers, or letters, will be positioned around five of the sides of a hexagon and you will be asked to provide the missing letter or number. The relationship between the numbers or letters may be with their corresponding number or letter on the opposite side of the hexagon, or it may follow in sequence from an adjacent number.

The decision is yours.

How to play

Key in the number, or letter, of your choice and press RETURN key.

Programming hints

This program has a tuner that displays the time in seconds on the screen while the computer is waiting for the player to key in something. This is a very useful facility and is done by setting the system variable TIME to zero at the start of the program. Time will then hold the time in seconds multiplied by 100. This can be displayed on occasions throughout the program but is more effective being displayed constantly, especially when the program is waiting for the player to key in something. This is done by using INKEY$ (10) in a loop which keeps checking if a key has been pressed and if it has not, it displays the time (see line 470). When a key has been found to be pressed, the program waits for the rest of the digits to be keyed and knows you have finished when the return key is pressed, i.e. GET$ = CHR$(13).

One change to make the puzzle easier, is to reduce the size of the numbers used. S(2) on line 150 is the value of the first number in the sequence if the pattern is a sequence of numbers going around the hexagon. IC on line 160 is related to the interval between the numbers going round the hexagon. So if the 9 in line 150 is changed to a smaller number and IC is always 1 this will make the puzzle easier.

If you wish to make the puzzle more difficult (and you must be brave or a genius to want to do so), then you could either increase the possible values of S(2) or IC or increase the number of different types of sequence. At present there are five different types of sequences depending on whether W is 0 to 4. If you allow W to become 5 or larger in line 170, you could add a new sequence type for W=5 after line 230.

```
10      REM HEXAGON PUZZLE
20      REM COPYRIGHT (C) G.LUDINSKI 1983
30      MODE 4
40      DIM S(8),IP$(255)
50      CLS
60      VDU 23,224,0,1,2,4,136,80,32,0
70      TE=0:CR=0:TIME=0
80      CLS
90      TE=TE+1
100     IF TE=11 OR TIME >= 20000 THEN GO
TO 670
110     REM
120     REM WORK OUT SEQUENCE
130     REM
140     S(1)=0
150     S(2)=INT(RND(1)*9+1)
160     IC=INT(RND(1)*4+1)
170     W=INT(RND(1)*5)
180     FOR I=3 TO 8
190        IF W=0 THEN S(I)=2*S(I-1)-S(I-2
)+IC:MS$="The interval increases by "+ST
R$(IC)+" each time"
200        IF W=1 THEN S(I)=S(I-1)+S(I-2)+
IC:MS$="Each number is the sum of the pr
evious two plus "+STR$(IC)
210        IF W=2 THEN S(I)=S(2)^(I-1):MS$
="Each number is "+STR$(S(2))+" to the p
ower of 2,3,4,5,6 and 7"
220        IF W=3 AND I > 5 THEN S(3)=S(2)
:S(4)=IC:S(5)=INT((S(2)+IC)/2):S(I)=S(2)
*S(I-3):MS$="Each number is "+STR$(S(2))
+" times the number     opposite it"
230        IF W=4 AND I > 5 THEN S(3)=S(2)
:S(4)=IC:S(5)=INT((S(2)+IC)/2):S(I)=IC*S
(11-I):MS$="The numbers on the left hand
 side of thewheel are "+STR$(IC)+" times
 the numbers on the    right hand side"
240        NEXT I
250     FOR I=1 TO 13:PRINT:NEXT I
260     REM
270     REM DISPLAY NUMBER WHEEL
280     REM
290     X1=640:Y1=704
300     X2=X1+259.81:Y2=Y1+150:Y3=Y1-150:
X3=X1-259.81
310     MOVE X1,Y1+300
320     DRAW X2,Y2
330     DRAW X2,Y3
340     DRAW X1,Y1-300
350     DRAW X3,Y3
360     DRAW X3,Y2
370     DRAW X1,Y1+300
380     DRAW X1,Y1-300
390     MOVE X2,Y2:DRAW X3,Y3
400     MOVE X2,Y3:DRAW X3,Y2
410     IF S(8) > 26 THEN LE=0:PRINT TAB(
21,5);S(3):PRINT TAB(23,10);S(4):PRINT T
AB(21,14);S(5):PRINT TAB(14,14);S(6):PRI
NT TAB(12,10);S(7)
420     IF S(8) <= 26 THEN LE=1:PRINT TA
B(21,5);CHR$(64+S(3)):PRINT TAB(23,10);C
```

```
HR$(64+S(4))):PRINT TAB(21,14);CHR$(64+S(
5))):PRINT TAB(18,14);CHR$(64+S(6))):PRINT
 TAB(16,10);CHR$(64+S(7))
    430   REM
    440   REM INPUT ANSWER
    450   REM
    460   IX=1
    470   IP$(IX)=INKEY$(10):IF IP$(IX)=""
THEN PRINT TAB(0,1);INT(TIME/100):GOTO 4
70
    480   PRINT TAB(IX+13,5);IP$(IX);:IX=IX
+1:IP$(IX)=GET$:IF IP$(IX) <> CHR$(13) T
HEN GOTO 480
    490   I$="":FOR I=1 TO IX-1:I$=I$+IP$(I
):NEXT I
    500   REM
    510   REM CHECK ANSWER
    520   REM
    530   *FX 15,1
    540   IF LE=0 AND ABS(VAL(I$) - S(8)) <
= LEN(I$)/2 THEN COLOUR1:VDU 8:PRINT TAB
(19,5);CHR$(224):CR=CR+1:COLOUR 3:GOTO 6
10
    550   IF LE=1 AND (I$=CHR$(64+S(8)) OR
 I$=CHR$(65+S(8))) THEN COLOUR1:VDU 8:PRI
NT TAB(19,5);CHR$(224):CR=CR+1:COLOUR 3:
GOTO 610
    560   PRINT TAB(0,21);"No,the answer =
 ";
    570   IF LE=0 THEN PRINT S(8)
    580   IF LE=1 THEN PRINT CHR$(64+S(8))
    590   IF LE=1 THEN PRINT:PRINT"Replace
 each letter by its position  number e
.9. 1 for A,2 for B etc."
    600   PRINT:PRINT MS$
    610   PRINT TAB(0,30);"Press Return to
 continue"
    620   INPUT A$
    630   GOTO 80
    640   REM
    650   REM SCORE SHEET
    660   REM
    670   CLS:PRINT
    680   PRINT"Number of puzzles    complet
ed = ";TE
    690   PRINT:PRINT"Number correct = ";CR
    700   PRINT:PRINT"Time taken = ";INT(TI
ME/100);" seconds"
    710   IQ=INT(CR*100/5.3)
    720   PRINT:PRINT"Your IQ level (numera
cy) = ";IQ
    730   PRINT
    740   IF CR >= 7 THEN PRINT"This is cla
ssed as SUPERIOR (upper 10%)":GOTO 770
    750   IF CR = 6 THEN PRINT"This is clas
sed as GOOD (upper 20%)":GOTO 770
    760   IF CR = 5 THEN PRINT"This is clas
sed as FAIR (upper 60%)"
    770   REM
```

SAFECRACKER

Are you a quick-thinker or a deep thinker? I hope you are one or the other, or you will never be able to crack open someone else's safe!

This game can be played two different ways, depending on whether you are a quick or deep thinker. If you are not sure which you are, then I suggest you play it both ways, and find out which way gives you the highest score.

In all cases, a closed safe is displayed and you are given two clues about the secret code that opens it. If you work out the exact answer before keying in the code, you are given 2 minutes to do it. If you make guesses, then you are only allowed 16 seconds. Wrong answers are ignored.

If you take too long you are surprised by the caretaker who switches on the light. He then presses the alarm button and you hear the police sirens wailing and you know all is lost.

If you do manage to crack the code in time, the safe opens, revealing gold bullion.

How to play

You are given two clues such as those shown above. The code is always a two digit number. Key in the number (you need not press RETURN).

To end the program, press E.

Programming hints

This program contains two useful procedures PROC BLOCK draws a rectangle whose lower left hand corner is X,Y and whose width is W and height is H. PROC__PARLL draws a parallelogram with two sides vertical. Put the coordinates of the lower, left-hand corner in X1, Y1 and those of the upper right hand corner in X2, Y2.

If you want to make the game easier, you can increase the time allowed to guess or reduce the number of digits allowed in the code or both.

To increase the time allowed for guesses, increase the value of TM in line 230. To increase the time allowed when only one answer is keyed in, increase the value of TM in line 210.

To reduce the number of digits allowed, reduce the number inside the RND brackets for XX and YY in line 510.

If you find the game too easy then do the opposite.

```
 10   REM SAFE CRACKER
 20   REM COPYRIGHT (C) G.LUDINSKI 1983
 30   MODE 5
 40   BL=0:RD=1:YE=2:WH=3:B=128
 50   SC=0
 60   TIME=0
 70   COLOUR BL+B:COLOUR WH
 80   CLS
 90   PRINT TAB(0,1);"Score":PRINT "  ";SC
100   REM
110   REM DRAW SAFE CLOSED
120   REM
130   GCOL 0,RD:PROC_BLOCK(0,0,1280,400)
140   GCOL 0,WH:PROC_BLOCK(400,350,400,600)
150   GCOL 0,BL:MOVE 450,400:DRAW 750,400:DRAW 750,900:DRAW 450,900:DRAW 450,400
160   COLOUR BL:COLOUR B+WH:PRINT TAB(10,12);"*"
170   PROC_QUESTION
180   COLOUR RD+B:COLOUR WH:PRINT TAB(0,22);"If you multiply the 1st digit by ";A1;" and the 2nd digit by ";ABS(B1);" and ";S1$;"   the result is ";C1;"."
190   PRINT"The 1st digit ";S2$
200   PRINT "the 2nd digit is ";C2:PRINT "What is the code"
210   TM=6000
220   I1$=INKEY$(0):IF TIME < TM AND I1$="" THEN GOTO 220
230   IF I1$ <> LEFT$(A$,1) AND I1$ <> "E" AND TIME < TM THEN TM=800:GOTO 220
240   IF I1$="E" THEN GOTO 700
250   IF TIME >= TM THEN GOTO 380
260   PRINT I1$;
270   I2$=INKEY$(0):IF TIME < TM AND I2$="" THEN GOTO 270
280   IF I2$ <> RIGHT$(A$,1) AND TIME < TM THEN GOTO 270
290   IF TIME >= TM THEN GOTO 380
300   PRINT I2$;
310   I$=I1$+I2$
320   IF I$=A$ THEN SC=SC+1:PROC_OPEN
330   PRINT " no,the code is ";A$
340   GOTO 60
350   REM
360   REM SWITCH LIGHT ON AND PLAY POLICE SIREN SOUNDS
370   REM
380   PRINT " no,the code is ";A$:VDU 19,BL,3,0,0,0:FORI=1TO6:SOUND1,-15,109,8:SOUND1,-15,101,8:NEXT:RB$=INKEY$(1000):VDU 19,BL,0,0,0,0:GOTO 60
390   REM
```

```
400   DEFPROC_BLOCK(X,Y,W,H)
410   MOVE X,Y:MOVE X+W,Y
420   PLOT 85,X,Y+H
430   PLOT 85,X+W,Y+H
440   ENDPROC
450   DEFPROC_PARLL(X,Y,X1,Y1,X2,Y2)
460   MOVE X,Y
470   MOVE X1,Y1:PLOT 85,X,Y+Y2-Y1
480   PLOT 85,X2,Y2
490   ENDPROC
500   DEFPROC_QUESTION
510   A1=RND(8)+1:B1=RND(8)+1:XX=RND(10
)-1:YY=RND(10)-1
520   W1=(-1)^RND(2):W2=(-1)^RND(2)
530   B1=B1*W1
540   C1=(A1*XX)+(B1*YY)
550   C2=XX+(W2*YY)
560   S1$="add them then":IF W1=-1 THEN
 S1$="subtract them"
570   S2$="plus":IF W2=-1 THEN S2$="min
us"
580   A$=STR$(ABS(XX))+STR$(ABS(YY))
590   ENDPROC
600   REM
610   REM DRAW SAFE OPEN
620   REM
630   DEFPROC_OPEN
640   GCOL 0,WH:PROC_PARLL(300,330,450,
400,450,900)
650   GCOL 0,BL:PROC_BLOCK(450,400,300,
500)
660   GCOL 0,YE:PROC_BLOCK(450,400,300,
200)
670   GCOL 0,BL:MOVE 300,330:DRAW 450,4
00:DRAW 450,900:DRAW 300,830
680   COLOUR B+BL:PRINT TAB(2,2);SC:RB$
=INKEY$(1000)
690   ENDPROC
700   END
```

FRACTIONS AND PERCENTAGES

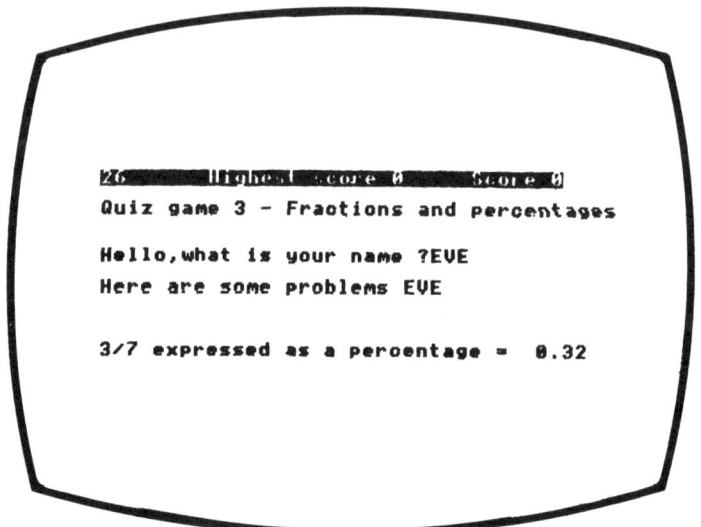

If you have trouble converting percentages to fractions and vice versa then this is for you.

How to play

The playing instructions are the same as those in the Profit and Loss program which is to be found elsewhere in this book.

Programming hints

The procedure PROC_CALC is a useful procedure

converting the computer into a calculator. It could be used on its own if a large number of calculations had to be made and a calculator was not at hand. It uses the keyword EVAL to evaluate the result of an expression contained in B$. B$ is the accumulated input.

The conversion from fraction to percentage routine expects the percentage value to be entered to two places of decimals i.e. it expects the player to key in 66.66 not 66.7. If the programmer requires more or fewer decimal places, then A$ in line 510 should be changed accordingly. The trick to write a number to a certain number of decimal places is to multiply it by 10 to the power of the number of decimal places you require, then find the integral part, then divide by the same number. In the program the fraction F/G is multiplied by a further 10 0 before conversion as the number is a percentage.

Even though the answer is given to a certain number of decimal places any answer, provided it is within 1 of the correct answer is accepted. This is so that the answer is marked correct however inaccurate the method used to obtain it. The most accurate method is to use the calculator routine provided but players may prefer to use mental arithmetic for speed.

Different types of problems can be added as described in Profit and Loss.

```
      10   REM  QUIZ            - FRACTIONS AND P
ERCENTAGES
      20   REM  COPYRIGHT  (C)  G.LUDINSKI  1983
      30   MODE  4
      40   DIM  IP$(255)
      50   S$="
                "
      52   HC$=" Highest score  ":HK$="          s
core "
      60     COLOUR 1:COLOUR 128:PRINT:PRINT:
PRINT:PRINT"Quiz game 3 - Fractions and
Percentages"
      80   PRINT:PRINT
      90   INPUT"Hello, what is your name ",N
AM$:PRINT:PRINT"Here are some problems "
  ;IF NAM$ <> "NO SOUND" THEN PRINTNAM$ E
LSE PRINT
```

```
100    W=1:C=0:T=1:I$="":TIME=0:P=0:MAX=0
102    P=P+1
104    PROC_QUESTION
106    PRINT:PRINT
110            PRINT:PRINTQ$" = ";:PROC_KEYIN:PRINT
120    IFI$="?"THEN PROC_CALC
130    IF W=-1 ANDI$=A$ AND I$<>"" THEN GOTO 160
140    IF W=1 AND ABS(VAL(I$)-VAL(A$))<1 AND I$<>"" THENGOTO160
150    GOTO 180
160      PRINT:PRINT"Yes,congratulations":C=C+1:PRINT:IF NAM$="NO SOUND" THEN GOTO 210
170    SOUND1,-10,12,10:SOUND1,-10,20,10:SOUND1,-10,28,10:SOUND1,-10,32,20:SOUND1,-10,14,20:GOTO 210
180    IF T=1 THEN PRINT:PRINT"No,"H$",try again":T=2:GOTO 110
190    PRINT:PRINT"Sorry,the answer is =":PRINT:PRINT L$:PRINT:PRINT M$
200    PRINT:PRINTN$
210    IF TIME >= 30000 THEN PROC_SCORE
220        PRINT:PRINT"Do you want more ?(Y/N)":PROC_KEYIN:PRINT
230        IF I$<>"Y" AND I$<>"N" AND I$<>"" AND I$<>"YES" AND I$<>"NO" THEN GOTO 220
240        IF I$="Y" OR I$="YES" OR I$="" THEN T=1:CLS:GOTO 102
242    PROC_SCORE
244    GOTO 9999
248    DEFPROC_QUESTION
250    L$="":M$="":N$="":B=40
260    W=-W:F=RND(9)
270    G=RND(9):J1=RND(19)
280    IF F=G OR F/G=INT(F/G) OR G/F = INT(G/F) THEN GOTO 260
290    IF F<G THEN E=INT(F/G*100):J=J1*5
300    IF G<F THEN E=INT(G/F*100):H=G:G=F:F=H:J=J1*2
310    E$=STR$(E):F$=STR$(F):G$=STR$(G):J$=STR$(J)
320    IF W=1 THEN GOTO 410
330    Q$=J$+"% converted into a fraction"
340    H$="P % is P/100. If top and bottom of    fraction are exactly divisible by the    same numbers,then divide by these    numbers"
350    HU=100:FOR I=1 TO 8
360        IF J/5 =INT(J/5) AND HU/5=INT(HU/5) THEN J=J/5:HU=HU/5
370        IF J/2=INT(J/2) AND HU/2=INT(HU/2) THEN J=J/2:HU=HU/2
380        NEXT I:A$=STR$(J)+"/"+STR$(HU)
390    L$=A$
400    M$="as "+J$+"/100 = "+A$
410    IF W=-1 THEN GOTO 460
420    Q$=F$+"/"+G$+" expressed as a percentage"
430    H$="P/Q is (P/Q) x 100 %"
440    A$=STR$(INT(F*10000/G)/100):L$=A$+"%"
450    M$="as ("+F$+"/"+G$+") x 100 = "+A$
460    ENDPROC
```

```
470 DEFPROC_CALC
480   VP=VPOS:PRINT TAB(0,22);"  Calculator mode           ";TAB(0,22)
490 B$=""
500 I$=GET$:PRINTI$;:B$=B$+I$:IFI$ <> "="ANDI$ <> "?"ANDB$<>"AC"THENGOTO500
510 IF B$="?"ORI$="?"THENGOTO550
520 IFB$="AC"THENPRINTTAB(0,23);S$;TAB(0,22):B$="":GOTO490
530 IFLEN(B$)<=1THENGOTO490
540 PRINTEVAL LEFT$(B$,LEN(B$)-1);TAB(0,22):GOTO490
550        PRINTTAB(0,22);S$;S$;TAB(0,VP-1):PROC_KEYIN
552 ENDPROC
560 DEFPROC_KEYIN
570 I%=1:VP=VPOS:HP=POS
572 IP$(I%)=INKEY$(10):IF IP$(I%)="" THEN COLOUR 0:COLOUR 129:PRINT TAB(0,1);INT(TIME/100);"       ";HC$;MAX;HK$;:COLOUR 1:COLOUR 128:GOTO 572
580     PRINT TAB(I%+HP,VP);IP$(I%);:I%=I%+1:IP$(I%)=GET$:IF IP$(I%) <> CHR$(13) THEN GOTO 580
590   I$="":FOR I=1 TO I%-1:I$=I$+IP$(I):NEXTI
600 ENDPROC
610 DEFPROC_SCORE
620 CLS
622 PRINT:PRINT
630 PRINT:PRINT"Number of problems completed = ";P
640 PRINT:PRINT"Number correct = ";C
650 TM=INT(TIME/100):PRINT:PRINT"Time taken in seconds = ";TM
660 IF C <> 0 THEN PRINT:PRINT"Time per problem in seconds = ";INT(TM/C)
670 IF C > MAX THEN MAX=C
680 TIME=0:P=0:C=0
690 ENDPROC
700 REM
9999 REM
```

A-MAZE-ING

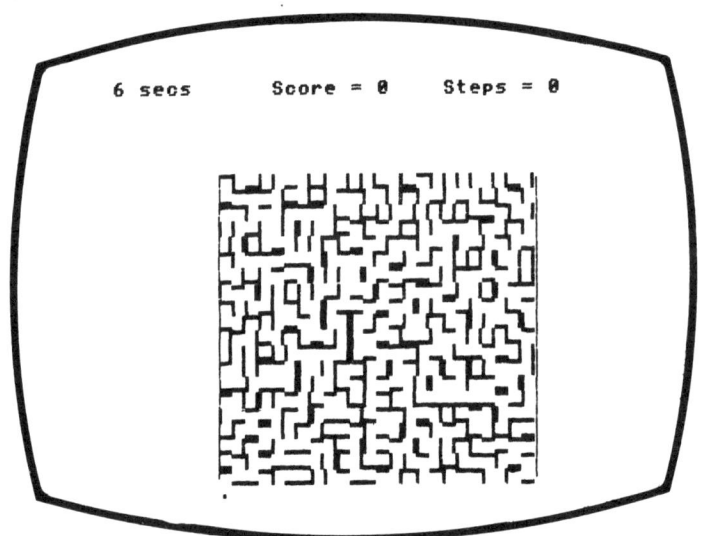

You are in the middle of a complicated maze, and your objective is to reach the outside in the quickest possible time, but also with the fewest number of moves possible.

Don't rush headlong into this one, as a little forward planning can save you time and points.

Every step counts as a point and every time you try to cross a barrier counts as a point.

You must aim for the top right hand corner or the exit nearest to that one.

How to play

You are represented by a dot in the lower left hand side of the maze, and you move by using the ARROW cursor keys.

Your score will be displayed at the top of the screen. The number of steps taken has a greater effect on your final score than the time factor.

You may, of course, retrace your steps and begin again from any point you wish to. When you have reached the outside, or you wish to give up, press the ESCAPE key.

We hope you make it, as there are plenty of other 'Brainteasers' waiting for you on the outside.

Programming hints

The maze is created of cells, each of which have one side blocked off. The cell shapes are drawn using VDU 23 to create user-defined graphics.

You could increase the size of the maze by changing 20 and 24 in lines 230 and 250. The maze shown is 24 columns wide by 20 rows. The maze array M% must be DIMensioned 1 column and 2 rows larger than the actual array to allow for checking for the (X+1)th column and (Y+1)th row. If you want the array in the centre of the screen you should change the PRINT statements in lines 220 and 240.

The lines drawn down the side of the maze in lines 300 and 310 would have to be changed, so would the start position of the dot in lines 320 and 330. In a 20 row maze the 21st row is the row the dot starts on, so special conditions apply to this row in lines 370 to 430. If a different number of rows is chosen this 21 must be changed.

```
10    REM A-MAZE-ING
20    REM COPYRIGHT (C) G.LUDINSKI 1983
22    ON ERROR RUN
30    MODE 4
40    DIM M%(25,22)
50    CLS:COLOUR 1:COLOUR 128
52    VDU 19,0,1,0,0,0
54    VDU 23;8202;0;0;0
60    LA$=CHR$(136):RA$=CHR$(137):DA$=C
HR$(138):UA$=CHR$(139)
70    GOTO 140
80    DEF FNB(N$)
90    TF=0
100   FOR L=0 TO 7
110     TF=TF+(2^L)*VAL(MID$(N$,8-L,1))
120   NEXT
130   =TF
140   VDU 23,224,3,3,3,3,3,3,3,3
150   VDU 23,225,0,0,0,0,0,0,255,255
160   VDU 23,226,192,192,192,192,192,19
2,192,192
170   VDU 23,227,255,255,0,0,0,0,0,0
180   VDU 23,228,3,3,3,FNB("00011011"),
FNB("00011011"),3,3,3
190   VDU 23,229,0,0,0,FNB("00011000"),
FNB("00011000"),0,255,255
200   VDU 23,230,192,192,192,FNB("11011
000"),FNB("11011000"),192,192,192
210   VDU 23,231,255,255,0,FNB("0001100
0"),FNB("00011000"),0,0,0
220   PRINT:PRINT:PRINT:PRINT:PRINT:PRI
NT
230   FOR I=1 TO 20
240     PRINT:PRINT "              ";
250     FOR J=1 TO 24
260       M%(J,I)=INT(RND(1)*4)
270       PRINT CHR$(224+M%(J,I));
280     NEXT:NEXT
300   MOVE 256,174:DRAW 256,790
310   MOVE 1028,174:DRAW 1028,790
320   ST=0:X=1:Y=21:X1=0:Y1=0:TIME=0
330   PRINT TAB(X+7,Y+6);".";CHR$(8);
340   *FX4,1
350   SC=ST+INT(TIME/500)
360   I$=INKEY$(0):IF I$="" OR I$ < CHR
$(136) OR I$ > CHR$(139) THEN PRINT TAB(
0,1);INT(TIME/100);" secs";TAB(12,1);"Sc
ore = ";SC;TAB(25,1);"Steps = ";ST:GOTO
360
370   IF (X=1 AND I$=LA$) OR (X=24 AND
I$=RA$) OR (Y=1 AND I$=UA$) OR (Y=21 AND
 I$=DA$) THEN GOTO 350
380   IF I$ = LA$ AND ((M%(X-1,Y) <> 0
AND M%(X,Y) <> 2 ) OR Y=21) THEN X=X-1
390   IF I$ = RA$ AND ((M%(X+1,Y) <> 2
AND M%(X,Y) <> 0) OR Y=21) THEN X=X+1
400   IF I$ = DA$ AND ((M%(X,Y+1) <> 3
AND M%(X,Y) <> 1) OR Y=21) THEN Y=Y+1
```

```
410 IF I$ = UA$ AND ((M%(X,Y-1) <> 1
AND M%(X,Y) <> 3) OR Y=21) THEN Y=Y-1
420   ST=ST+1
430   IF Y=21 THEN PRINT TAB(X+7,27);".
"; :GOTO 450
440   PRINT TAB(X+7,Y+6);CHR$(M%(X,Y)+2
28);CHR$(8);
450   IF X=X1 AND Y=Y1 THEN SOUND 1,-15
,53,10
460   X1=X:Y1=Y
470   GOTO 350
```

SAINTS TO SINNERS

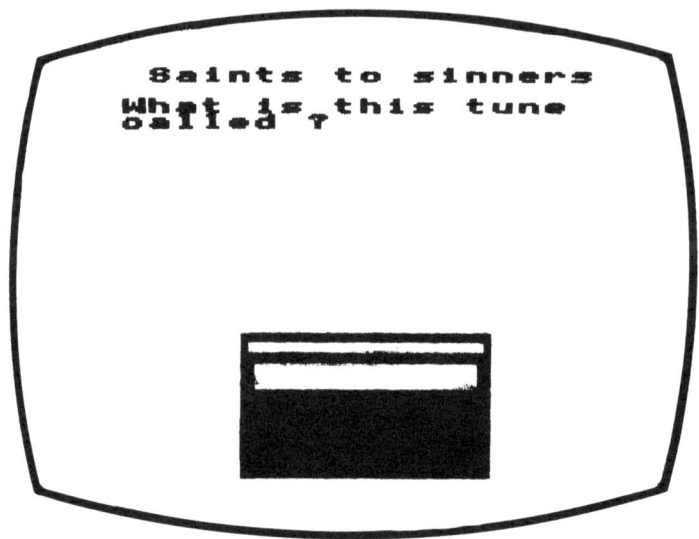

Here is a musical test for the members of your family who have a keen ear for a tune.

The object of the game is to guess the tune being played and to make it easy, to begin with, we have allowed your computer to play the entire tune. After the first ten 'numbers' you will only hear a short snatch from the tune.

We have included a very large selection of tunes suitable for 'saints and sinners'.

To make life more difficult for the player we have entered the tunes, using a special code, so that they cannot be guessed at in advance.

How to play

When you think that you have guessed, correctly, the title of the tune being played, type in the full title press RETURN and find out if your ear is musical, or tin.

Programming hints

Lines 200-480 contains the procedure that plays the tune. The notes of the tune are held in the first and second, if any, elements of the array A$ and the name of the tune is held in N$. W is the indicator determining which tune is to be played. The tune stored in array A$ is terminated by the letters XXXXX. If more than one element of the array is needed to store the tune, the first element is terminated by the letters NNNNN. Storing data in a string variable is a very useful trick when there are too many fields to be assigned to use assignment statements, and when you do not wish to use DATA statements, as you will be accessing data randomly, not sequentially. See the section entitled Possible alterations for further details.

The obvious alterations that can be made, are that when you know the names of the tunes you will want to change them. If you wish to increase the number of tunes that can be played then you must increase the maximum value of W held in line 100. You could then include your tune between 380 and 390 starting with a statement ensuring that the tune is skipped over if the value of W is not the correct one. You could then work out the tune your require on an instrument, or else you could copy a musical score. If you are copying a musical score then you should refer to the User Guide, but if you are doing it for fun then I recommend a child's musical instrument which usually just has the octave which starts with middle C which is the most common octave. The pitch numbers for this octave are:

Middle C 053
        D 061
        E 069
        F 073
        G 081
        A 089
        B 097
        C 101

The duration of the notes should be smaller numbers than specified in the User Guide as processing the array takes time. Therefore I suggest that the durations should be 03,08 and 18 approximately for notes of short, middle or long duration. When you have worked out the pitch and duration of all the notes, you should assign them to the first and, if more room is required, the second element of the array. The pitch number must have three digits and the duration must have two and they should be joined together and separated from details of the next note by a space. As stated before, the first element is terminated by NNNNN and the second element by XXXXX.

I do not expect you will bother to put the name of the tune in code, but in case you do N$ is made up of the ASCII values of the letters of the name of the tune, remembering to include spaces which have an ASCII value of 32. If you do not bother to code the name of the tune, assign the name to NAM$ and make sure the program skips line 120.

```
 10   REM SAINTS TO SINNERS
 20   REM COPYRIGHT (C) G.LUDINSKI 1983
 30   MODE 5
 40   DIM A$(2)
 50   NT=0
 60   CLS
 70   NT=NT+1
 80   PRINT:PRINT " Saints to sinners"
 90   PROC_RADIO
100   W=INT(RND(1)*5)
```

```
110    PROC_TUNE(W)
120    NAM$="":FOR I=1 TO LEN(N$) STEP 2
:NAM$=NAM$+CHR$(VAL(MID$(N$,I,2))):NEXT
I
130    PRINT:PRINT"What is this tune   c
alled ?":PRINT
140    INPUT I$
150    IF I$=NAM$ THEN PRINT:PRINT"You a
re right":GOTO 170
160    PRINT:PRINT"No,it is called ":PRI
NT NAM$
170    PRINT:PRINT"Do you want more Y/N"
180    INPUT I$:IF I$="Y" OR I$="" THEN
GOTO 60
190    GOTO 610
200    DEFPROC_TUNE(W)
210    A$(1)="":A$(2)="":N$=""
220    IF W <> 0 THEN GOTO 250
230    A$(1)="06105 08115 08915 09725 00
005 09705 10110 10105 09710 08105 09710
08910 00005 06105 06920 07720 08110 0890
5 09705 06910 08915 10105 09720 08920 08
125 00005 XXXXX "
240    N$="8076657383738232683965777985 8
2"
250    IF W <> 1 THEN GOTO 290
260    A$(1)=STRING$(2,"05310 06110 0691
0 05310 00010 ")+STRING$(2,"06910 07310
08120 00005 ")+"NNNNN "
270    A$(2)=STRING$(2,"08105 08905 0810
5 07305 06910 05310 00010 ")+STRING$(2,"
05310 04110 05320 00010 ")+"XXX"
280    N$="7082698269327465678185698 3"
290    IF W <> 2 THEN GOTO 320
300    A$(1)="06905 06105 05310 06105 06
905 07305 08110 00005 08905 09705 10110
09710 08910 08110 00010 08905 09705 1011
0 09710 08910 08110 08910 09710 10110 08
110 07310 06910 00010 XXXXX "
310    N$="8472632707382828343278796976"
320    IF W <> 3 THEN GOTO 350
330    A$(1)="05310 06910 07320 00005 07
305 00001 07305 06905 07305 08110 00001
08110 07320 00005 07310 08910 10110 0000
5 08905 00001 08905 08105 07302 00001 07
302 06905 07320 XXXXX "
340    N$="79786769327378328279896576326
86586736839833267738489"
350    IF W <> 4 THEN GOTO 390
360    A$(1)="06905 00001 06905 07310 08
120 00001 07305 06905 06110 00001 06110
06905 00001 06905 07310 08120 00010 0690
5 00001 06905 07310 08120 00001 07305 06
905 06110 00001 06110 06905 00001 06905
07310 08920 NNNNN "
370    A$(2)="00010 08110 08910 10120 00
001 10105 09705 08910 00001 08910 00005
08105 07305 06910 00001 06910 XXX"
380    N$="74693284396573776 9"
390    IF NT > 10 THEN A$(1)=RIGHT$(A$(1
),6*INT(RND(1)*17+3))
400    FOR J=1 TO 2
410      FOR I=1 TO 255 STEP 6
420        IF MID$(A$(J),I,3) = "NNN" TH
EN I=255:GOTO 460
430        IF MID$(A$(J),I,3) = "XXX" TH
EN I=255:J=2:GOTO 460
440        IF MID$(A$(J),I,3)="000" THEN
```

```
       SOUND 1,0,0,VAL(MID$(A$(J),I+3,2)):GOTO
       460
       450       SOUND 1,-15,VAL(MID$(A$(J),I,
3)),VAL(MID$(A$(J),I+3,2))
       460       NEXT I
       470     NEXT J
       480   ENDPROC
       490   DEFPROC_RADIO
       500   GCOL 0,1:PROCBLOCK(300,150,600,25
0)
       510   GCOL 0,2:PROCBLOCK(330,330,540,50
)
       520   GCOL 0,3:PROCBLOCK(300,400,10,30)
       530   PROCBLOCK(300,430,600,10)
       540   PROCBLOCK(890,400,10,30)
       550   ENDPROC
       560   DEFPROCBLOCK(X,Y,W,H)
       570   MOVE X,Y:MOVE X+W,Y
       580   PLOT 85,X,Y+H
       590   PLOT 85,X+W,Y+H
       600   ENDPROC
       610   REM
```

SPOT THE DIFFERENCE

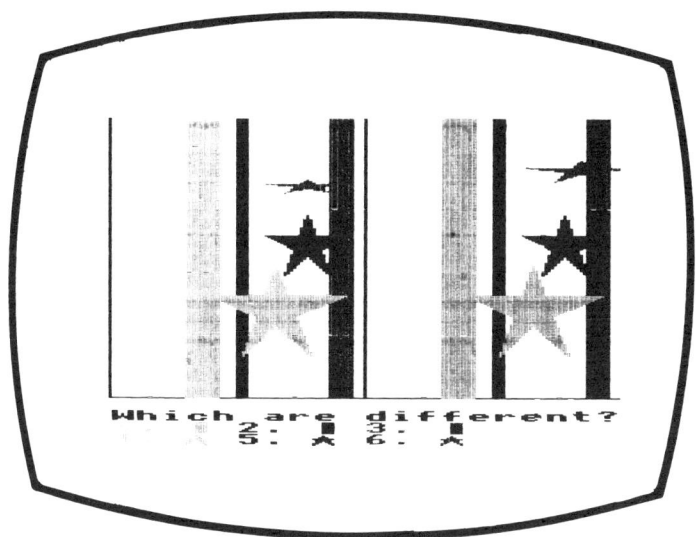

I suppose that this could have been called Star and Stripe, the difference as you will see when you run this colourful eye test.

Two pictures, composed of stars and stripes, in red, white and blue appear on the screen, and you will be asked to identify which of the items is different.

How to play

Items are keyed as follows:

>Red Stripe 1
>White stripe 2
>Blue stripe 3

Red star   4
White star 5
Blue star   6

Identify the differences and key in the number and press RETURN. If you are correct you will hear a high pitched tune, but if you are wrong your answer will be crossed.

To help you, numbers previously keyed in are displayed in brackets. When all the numbers required have been keyed in a further tune will be played. Just hope that it is high pitched for a correct answer.

To continue, or stop, press Y or N and RETURN.

At conclusion you will see your score sheet showing tries, correct answers, and time/average taken.

Programming hints

You might find the routine P ROC_STAR useful in your non-commercial programs as it draws a star. You just have to specify the bottom left-hand corner of the star (X,Y), the width of the bottom of the star (W), the height of the star (H) and the COLOUR that it is to be displayed in (CL).

You could make the puzzle easier by increasing the range of possible values for the shapes that are going to be different. The function FNM (MIN, MAX) is used to define the minimum and maximum value of any shape. Remember if you increase the MAX value you must reduce MIN by the same value, or the picture will extend beyond the allocated area.

```
10  REM SPOT THE DIFFERENCE
20  REM COPYRIGHT (C) G.LUDINSKI 1983
30  MODE 5
```

```
40      DIM WH(6),AN$(6)
50      VDU 19,2,4,0,0,0
60      TIME=0:CR=0:NQ=0
70      GOTO 240
80      REM
90      REM RANDOM NUMBER IN RANGE
100     REM
110     DEF FNM(MIN,MAX)=INT((MAX-MIN)*RN
D(1)+MIN)
120     REM
130     REM U.D.G. CALCULATOR
140     REM
150     DEF FNB(N$)
160     TF=0
170     FOR L=0 TO 7
180       TF=TF+(2^L)*VAL(MID$(N$,8-L,1))
190     NEXT L
200     =TF
210     REM
220     REM STARS AND STRIPES
230     REM
240     VDU 23,224,30,30,30,30,30,30,30,30
250     VDU 23,225,0,FNB("00010000"),FNB(
"00111000"),FNB("11111110"),FNB("0111110
0"),FNB("01101100"),FNB("11000110"),FNB(
"10000010")
260     RI$=CHR$(224):ST$=CHR$(225)
270     REM
280     REM START
290     REM
300     CLS
310     NQ=NQ+1
320     REM
330     REM FRAMEWORK
340     REM
350     GCOL 0,3:COLOUR 3:COLOUR 128
360     MOVE 0,256:DRAW 1279,256
370     DRAW 1279,1023:DRAW 0,1023:DRAW 0
,256
380     MOVE 640,256:DRAW 640,1023
390     REM
400     REM DRAW PATTERNS
410     REM
420     NZ=0
430     FOR I=1 TO 6
440       WH(I)=INT(2*RND(1))
450       IF WH(I)=1 THEN NZ=NZ+1
460     NEXT I
470     IF NZ=0 THEN GOTO 430
480     FOR S=0 TO 1
490       FOR J=1 TO 3
500         IF S<>0 THEN GOTO 580
510         X=FNM(J*160-80,160*(J+1)-80)
520         W=FNM(20,80)
530         IJ=J
540         CL=J:IF J=2 THEN CL=3
550         IF J=3 THEN CL=2
560         PROC_STRIPE(X,W,CL)
570         PROC_STRIPE(X+640+(WH(IJ)*FNM
(20,40)),W+(WH(IJ)*FNM(20,40)),CL)
580         IF S<>1 THEN GOTO 680
590         X=FNM(160,480)
600         Y=FNM(256,896)
610         W=FNM(80,2*(640-X)/3)
620         H=FNM(128,768-Y)
630         IJ=J+3
640         CL=J:IF J=2 THEN CL=3
```

25

```
650         IF J=3 THEN CL=2
660         PROC_STAR(X,Y,W,H,CL)
670         PROC_STAR(X+640+(WH(IJ)*FNM(2
0,40)),Y+(WH(IJ)*FNM(20,40)),W+(WH(IJ)*F
NM(20,40)),H+(WH(IJ)*FNM(20,40)),CL)
680         NEXT J
690       NEXT S
700     REM
710     REM QUESTION
720     REM
730     PRINT TAB(0,25);"Which are differ
ent?";:COLOUR 1:PRINT "   1. ";RI$;:COLO
UR 3:PRINT " 2. ";RI$;:COLOUR 2:PRINT "
3. ";RI$
740     COLOUR 1:PRINT "   4. ";ST$;:COLO
UR 3:PRINT " 5. ";ST$;:COLOUR 2:PRINT "
6. ";ST$
750     PROC_ANSWER
760     COLOUR 3
770     IR$=""
780     FOR I=1 TO (LEN(A$)+1)/2
790       I$=INKEY$(0):IF I$="" THEN GOTO
 790
800       PRINT I$;" (";IR$;")";
810       KI=0
820       FOR K=1 TO NA
830         IF I$=AN$(K) THEN AN$(K)="0":
KI=1:SOUND 1,-15,101,10:IR$=IR$+I$
840       NEXT K
850       IF KI=0 THEN PRINT " X" ELSE PR
INT
860       RB$=INKEY$(100):VDU 11:PRINT "
        ":VDU 11
870     NEXT I
880     FOR I=1 TO NA
890       IF AN$(I) <> "0" THEN GOTO 920
900     NEXT I
910     GOTO 930
920     PRINT "No,ans.=";A$:SOUND 1,-15,7
3,10:SOUND 1,-15,69,5:GOTO 940
930     PRINT "Yes,you are right":SOUND 1
,-15,101,30:CR=CR+1
940     PRINT"Do you want more Y/N";
950     INPUT R$
960     IF R$ <> "N" THEN GOTO  300
970     REM
980     REM SCORE SHEET
990     REM
1000    CLS:PRINT:PRINT"Spot the differen
ce":FOR I=1 TO 9:PRINT:NEXTI
1010    PRINT:PRINT"Puzzles attempted=";N
Q
1020    PRINT:PRINT"Puzzles correct=";CR
1030    PRINT:PRINT"Time taken=";INT(TIME
/100):PRINT "secs"
1040    IF CR <> 0 THEN PRINT:PRINT"Time/
puzzle=";INT(TIME/(CR*100)):PRINT "secs"
1050    GOTO 1290
1060    DEFPROC_STRIPE(X,W,CL)
1070    GCOL 0,CL
1080    MOVE X,256:MOVE X+W,256
1090    PLOT 85,X,1024
1100    PLOT 85,X+W,1024
1110    ENDPROC
1120    DEFPROC_STAR(X,Y,W,H,CL)
1130    GCOL 0,CL
1140    MOVE X+(W/2),Y+(H/3)
1150    MOVE X,Y:PLOT 85,X+(W/2),Y+H
```

```
1160    MOVE X+(W/2),Y+(H/3)
1170    MOVE X+W,Y:PLOT 85,X+(W/2),Y+H
1180    MOVE X+(W/2),Y+(H/3)
1190    MOVE X-(W/2),Y+(2*H/3):PLOT 85,X+
(3*W/2),Y+(2*H/3)
1200    ENDPROC
1210    DEFPROC_ANSWER
1220    A$="":IM=0
1230    FOR L=1 TO 6
1240      IF WH(L)=1 THEN IM=IM+1:AN$(IM)
=STR$(L):A$=A$+STR$(L)+","
1250      NEXT L
1260    A$=LEFT$(A$,LEN(A$)-1)
1270    NA=IM
1280    ENDPROC
1290    REM
```

RELATIONS

```
            Relations

        5  3  5  6
        3  2  1  2
        8  2  5  7   16
        7  1  8  7

    combine a row or column to be
        equal to the red number
        Use + - * / ∧ SQR < >
```

This following program is one where you should deny yourself, and any other player, the use of paper and pencil if you really want some mental exercise.

The screen will display a four by four matrix of numbers, to the left hand side. On the right hand side will be shown a number, or numbers, in red.

You have to combine two, or more, of the numbers in any of the rows to arrive at the same figure as the red number/s.

How to play

To reach your answer you may use any of the following operators:

> + plus
> − minus
> * multiplication
> / division
> ∧ to the power of
> SQR square root of

Example: If the red number is 1 and the row is 9 2 4 8 the solution would be

> SQR (9) + 2 − 4

This, followed by RETURN, would give 1 as it's answer.

Correct answers will mean that you will be asked if you wish to proceed. Answer Y or No followed by RETURN.

If you answer incorrectly your computer will explain, and show, the correct solution.

A score sheet appears after 200 seconds which will show your results and give an IQ rating against your reasoning powers.

Programming hints

The matrix is displayed in double height, double width characters. This is done by using Mode 5 to give double width characters and then defining 20 user defined characters which consist of the top halves of the numbers 0 to 9 and the bottom halves of numbers 0 to 9.

The pattern for the numbers 0 to 9 is found by calling the OSWORD routine with the hexadecimal number A in the accumulator (%A). The OSWORD routine is at &FFF1. See the user guide for further details if you are not familiar with machine code or the ROM routines.

If you wish to increase the number of rows or columns of the matrix then you must change the maximum value of I (row) or J (column) in the FOR...NEXT loops.

```
  10   REM RELATIONS
  20   REM COPYRIGHT (C) G.LUDINSKI 1983
  30   REM ON ERROR PROC_ERROR:GOTO 830
  40   MODE 5
  50   DIM A(4,4),X(16),Y(16)
  60   CLS
  70   REM
  80   REM CREATE DOUBLE HEIGHT CHARACTERS
  90   REM
 100   A%=&A
 110   X%=0:Y%=&A
 120   FOR I=0 TO 9
 130     ?&A00=ASC(STR$(I))
 140     CALL (&FFF1)
 150     VDU 23,224+(2*I),?&A01,?&A01,?&A02,?&A02,?&A03,?&A03,?&A04,?&A04
 160     VDU 23,224+(2*I)+1,?&A05,?&A05,?&A06,?&A06,?&A07,?&A07,?&A08,?&A08
 170   NEXT I
 180   TIME=0:NO=0:CR=0
 190   REM
 200   REM GENERATE NUMBERS
 210   REM
 220   CLS
 230   PRINT:PRINT "      Relations"
 240   PRINT:PRINT
 250   IF TIME >= 20000 THEN GOTO 890
 260   NO=NO+1
 270   FOR I=1 TO 4
 280     FOR J=1 TO 4
 290       A(I,J)=RND(9)
 300     NEXT J
 310   NEXT I
 320   REM
 330   REM DISPLAY NUMBERS
 340   REM
 350   COLOUR 128:COLOUR 2
 360   FOR I=1 TO 4
 370     PRINT
 380     FOR T=1 TO 2
 390       FOR J=1 TO 4
 400         IF T=1 THEN PRINT " ";CHR$(224+(2*A(I,J)));
 410         IF T=2 THEN PRINT " ";CHR$(224+(2*A(I,J))+1);
 420       NEXT J
 430       PRINT
 440     NEXT T
 450   NEXT I
```

```
460   REM
470   REM GENERATE RED NUMBER
480   REM
490   S1=RND(2):S2=INT(RND(1)*10):SM=VA
L(STR$(S1)+STR$(S2))
500   COLOUR 1
510   PRINT TAB(13,9);CHR$(224+(2*S1));
CHR$(224+(2*S2))
520   PRINT TAB(13,10);CHR$(224+(2*S1)+
1);CHR$(224+(2*S2)+1)
530   COLOUR 3
540   REM
550   REM CHECK ANSWER
560   REM
570   PRINT TAB(0,17);"Combine a row or
   column to be equal to the red numbe
r"
580   PRINT
590   PRINT "Use + - * / ^ SQR ( )"
600   PRINT
610   INPUT I$
620   IF I$="" THEN PROC_ERROR:GOTO 830
630   IF EVAL(I$) <> SM THEN PRINT:PRIN
T"No,they are not = ";SM:GOTO 830
640   N$=""
650   FOR I=1TO LEN(I$)
660     NU$=MID$(I$,I,1)
670     IF NU$ >= "0" AND NU$ <= "9" TH
EN N$=N$+NU$
680   NEXT I
690   IF LEN(N$) > 4 OR LEN(N$) = 0 THE
N PROC_ERROR:GOTO 830
700   SG$=""
710   FOR T=1 TO 2
720     FOR I=1 TO 4
730       SG$=SG$+"X"
740       FOR J=1 TO 4
750         IF T=1 THEN SG$=SG$+STR$(A(
I,J))
760         IF T=2 THEN SG$=SG$+STR$(A(
J,I))
770       NEXT J
780     NEXT I
790     SG$=SG$+"X"
800   NEXT T
810   IF INSTR(SG$,N$)=0 THEN PROC_ERRO
R:GOTO 830
820   PRINT:PRINT"Yes,you are right":CR
=CR+1
830   PRINT:PRINT"Do you want more Y/N"
;
840   INPUT R$
850   IF R$ <> "N" THEN GOTO 220
860   REM
870   REM SCORE SHEET
880   REM
890   CLS
900   TM=TIME/100
910   PRINT:PRINT"Number of Problems ="
;NO
920   PRINT:PRINT"Number correct = ";CR
930   PRINT:PRINT"Time taken = ";INT(TM
):PRINT"secs"
940   IQ=INT((CR*100)/5.3):IF IQ > 150
THEN IQ=150
950   PRINT:PRINT"IQ level (reasoning)=
";IQ
960   IF CR >= 7 THEN PRINT:PRINT"This
is SUPERIOR   (upper 10%)":GOTO 1030
```

```
 970    IF CR = 6 THEN PRINT:PRINT"This i
s GOOD (upper 30%)":GOTO 1030
 980    IF CR >= 4 THEN PRINT:PRINT"This
is FAIR (upper 60%)":GOTO 1030
 990    GOTO 1030
1000    DEFPROC_ERROR
1010    PRINT TAB(0,26);"Error, wrong numb
ers"
1020    ENDPROC
1030    REM
```

N.B. In lines 110 — 160 inclusive, you will see & and ?. Do not confuse these with numbers 8 and 7.

DON'T PAINT THE CAT

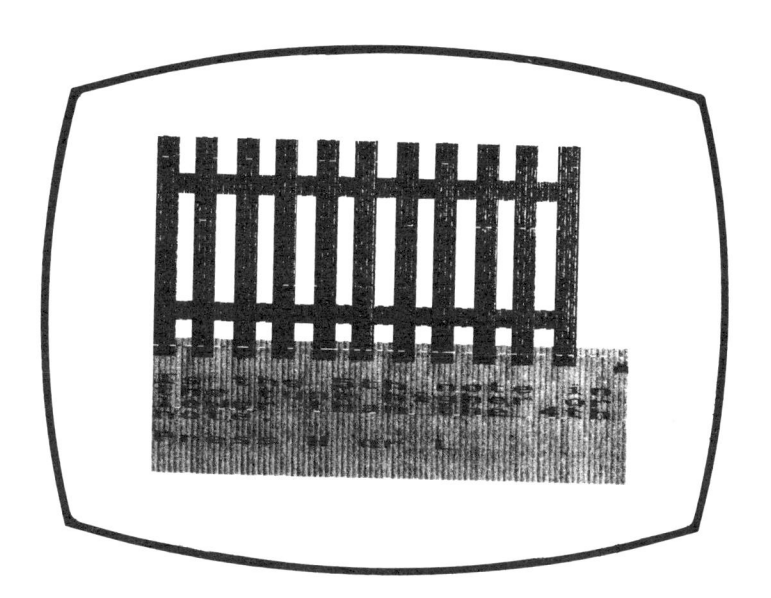

Seems a strange title for a program. I mean, who would want to emulsion paint the family mogg anyway?

Well you see, the family have decided that you have to paint the garden fence. You lost the draw — it might have been your sister instead who had to do it, but never mind there is always next time. Across the fence from you and your fantastic paint brush, is your neighbour's transistor. As a mental challenge you have decided to paint the fence according to the high/low pitch of your neighbour's music.

Look out for your cat, it's parked at the end of the fence.

How to play

As the game begins you will hear just two notes to compare but, everytime you get the answer correct the next tune will have an extra note.

You will be told which two notes to compare, and you must key in H or L for High or Low.

If you get it wrong you must wait for the fence, and the poor old pussy, to be painted.

If you take too long to answer, the cat will wind up getting covered in paint anyway.

Press the RETURN key when you want a new tune.

Programming hints

If you can work out the answer long before the cat is painted, then reduce the 50 of INKEY$(50) in line 540.

If you find that it is too difficult to tell the difference between the notes, then increase the 5 after the '*' sign in line 470.

Alternatively you can increase the time allowed to answer, or reduce the difference between the notes, by doing the opposite of what is described above.

```
 10    REM DON'T PAINT THE CAT
 20    REM COPYRIGHT (C) G.LUDINSKI 1983
 30    MODE 5
 40     DIM N(10)
 50    CLS
 60    VDU 19,0,4,0,0,0,19,2,2,0,0,0
 70    GOTO 200
 80    REM
 90    REM U.D.G. CALCULATOR
100    REM
110    DEF FNB(N$)
120    TF=0
```

```
130     FOR L=0 TO 7
140       TF=TF+(2^L)*VAL(MID$(N$,8-L,1))
150     NEXT L
160     =TF
170   REM
180   REM CAT SHAPE
190   REM
200   VDU 23,224,FNB("01010000"),FNB("0
1110000"),FNB("01110000"),FNB("11111000"
),FNB("11111000"),FNB("11111000"),255,FN
B("10001000")
210   REM
220   REM DRAW FENCE
230   REM
240   FOR J=2 TO 9
250     COLOUR 128:CLS
260     GCOL 0,2:PROC_BLOCK(0,0,1280,45
0)
270     GCOL 0,3
280     FOR I=0 TO 1000 STEP 100
290       PROC_BLOCK(I,400,50,600)
300     NEXT I
310     PROC_BLOCK(0,500,1050,50):PROC_
BLOCK(0,850,1050,50)
320     COLOUR 3:COLOUR 130:PRINT TAB(1
8,19);CHR$(224)
330     COLOUR 3:COLOUR 130
340     W1=RND(J):W2=RND(J):IF W1 = W2
THEN GOTO 340
350     T1$="th":T2$="th":IF W1=1 THEN
T1$="st"
360     T2$="th":IF W2=1 THEN T2$="st"
370     IF W1=2 THEN T1$="nd"
380     IF W2=2 THEN T2$="nd"
390     IF W1=3 THEN T1$="rd"
400     IF W2=3 THEN T2$="rd"
410     PRINT TAB(0,21);"Is the ";W1;T1
$;" note in the tune higher or lower t
han the ";W2;T2$;" note.":PRINT:PRINT"P
ress H or L ";
420     N(0)=0
430     FOR K=1 TO J
440       REM
450       REM PLAY THE TUNE
460       REM
470       N(K)=INT(RND(5)*5+50):IF N(K)
=N(K-1) THEN GOTO 470
480       IF J=2 AND N(1)>=N(2) THEN GOT
O 470
490       SOUND 1,-15,N(K),10:SOUND 1,0
,0,1
500     NEXT K
510     IF N(W1) > N(W2) THEN A$="H"
520     IF N(W1) < N(W2) THEN A$="L"
530     GCOL 0,1:I=-100:I$="":ID=0
540     I$=INKEY$(50):IF I$="" OR ID=1
THEN I=I+100:PROC_BLOCK(I,400,50,600):IF
 I < 1000 THEN GOTO 540
550     IF I$=A$ AND ID=0 THEN PRINT:PR
INT:PRINT"Yes,you are right":GOTO 600
560     IF I < 1000 THEN PRINT I$;:ID=1
:GOTO 540
570     COLOUR 1:PRINT TAB(18,19);CHR$(
224):SOUND1,-1,80,1:SOUND0,-15,7,20:COLO
UR 3
580     IF A$="H" THEN PRINT TAB(0,28);
"No,it is higher (H)"
590     IF A$="L" THEN PRINT TAB(0,28);
"No,it is lower (L)"
```

```
600     COLOUR 3:PRINT TAB(0,30);"Hit R
eturn for more";:INPUT RB$
610     IF I$ <> A$ THEN GOTO 250
620     NEXT J
630    PRINT TAB(0,27);"A musician like
   yourself should'nt  be painting fenc
es !":GOTO 700
640    REM
650    DEFPROC_BLOCK(X,Y,W,H)
660    MOVE X,Y:MOVE X+W,Y
670    PLOT 85,X,Y+H
680    PLOT 85,X+W,Y+H
690    ENDPROC
700    END
```

FRANCIS DRAKE ADVENTURE GAME

This is by far and away the most ambitious, interesting and testing program in this book.

This is an authentic historical adventure game based on Francis Drake's circumnavigation of the world, from 1577 to 1580. As you travel in the footsteps of the greatest of Elizabeth the First's free-booting adventurers, you will encounter the same problems and challenges as Drake.

Drake sailed in search of the elusive North West Passage that would allow him access to the Pacific, and the galleons of the Spanish Empire. As history books will already have told you, he did not find the object of his quest, but he did find much more, and so will you as you sail into the Francis Adventure Game.

How to play

Because of the complexity of this adventure the program has been split into two parts. This is because of the limitations of memory, but it will also mean that you do not have to complete entering the program at one sitting. You will have to store both halves on the same side of the tape, if you are 'saving', and, obviously, in the correct order.

Allow a slight gap between the two programs.

Load and run the first program but leave the PLAY button depressed so that the second program will run when loaded.

The first program displays the title and map which can be checked before proceeding.

The second program consists of the text. To test this half Key in MODE 1 : CLS press RETURN.

When the program has been loaded and RUN, you will hear the gentle lapping of waves against the shore.

On the map you will see your position marked by a white sailing ship, docked near the port of Lima.

Everytime you use this game, the dangers and treasures will be located in different parts of the ocean, so do not think that you can predict your moves too easily. We didn't feel it was fair, however, to move the rocks, reefs and Spanish galleons, so try and remember their locations. It will help you considerably.

You **must** follow Drake's route by first travelling to the port known as New Albion and thence onward, past Java, to the bottom left hand corner of the map.

Your aim is to reach the bottom of the map with, at least, four times the amount of the cargo with which you began.

If you achieve this feat of daring then you will, naturally, be rewarded by the gift of a knighthood from your grateful, and avaricious, Queen.

You move using the ARROW cursor keys.

If you input wrong information (or information the computer does not understand) then the cursor stays on the same line but moves to the left and waits for accurate information. If you key in correct information the cursor moves upwards to under the map.

At intervals you will be told the situation at sea and asked which action you would like to take, from the choice shown.

Remember to consider your options carefully as to the amounts of cargo, supplies, cannon balls and crew conditions.

Damage rating is based on a 1 to 10 scale. If you are damaged to the level of 10 then I'm afraid that it's into the sea for you, as the Golden Hind settles gently below your feet.

Do your best, as the present Government is emptying the coffers more quickly than you are filling them.

Hints and changes you can make

One of the problems of displaying a map on the screen, is how to reduce the memory required and the number of lines needed to describe the map. This is done here by defining a string array M$, with the number of elements being equal to the number of rows on the map. Standard shapes are then defined using VDU 23. The shapes are as shown below:

225 226 227 228 229 230 231 232 233

Each row of the map is assigned to an element of M$ using the above shapes, and zero (to represent blanks). Each shape is described as a single digit by subtracting 224 from its shape number. This is displayed using CHR$ (224 + (shape number -224)).

If you find the adventure too easy, then reduce the cargo (CA), supplies (SU), crew (CR), and/or cannon balls (BA) that you start with. They are on line 410. If you find that knighthood escapes you, then reduce the 400 in line 480.

```
10    REM FRANCIS DRAKE ADVENTURE GAME
20    REM COPYRIGHT (C) G.LUDINSKI 1983
30    MODE 5
40    PROC_TITLE
50    MODE 1
60    DIM M$(17)
70    VDU 19,1,4,0,0,0,19,2,2,0,0,0
80    COLOUR 129:COLOUR 2
90    CLS
100   GOTO 170
110   DEF FNB(N$)
120   TF=0
130   FOR L=0 TO 7
140     TF=TF+(2^L)*VAL(MID$(N$,8-L,1))
150   NEXT L
160   =TF
170   VDU 23,225,255,255,255,255,0,0,0,0
180   VDU 23,226,0,0,0,0,255,255,255,255
190   B1=FNB("11110000"):VDU 23,227,B1,B1,B1,B1,B1,B1,B1,B1
200   B1=FNB("00001111"):VDU 23,228,B1,B1,B1,B1,B1,B1,B1,B1
210   Z1=FNB("11111110"):Z2=FNB("11111100"):Z3=FNB("11111000"):Z4=FNB("11110000"):Z5=FNB("11100000"):Z6=FNB("11000000"):Z7=FNB("10000000")
220   L1=FNB("01111111"):L2=FNB("00111111"):L3=FNB("00011111"):L4=FNB("00001111"):L5=FNB("00000111"):L6=FNB("00000011"):L7=FNB("00000001")
230   VDU 23,229,255,Z1,Z2,Z3,Z4,Z5,Z6,Z7
240   VDU 23,230,L7,L6,L5,L4,L3,L2,L1,255
```

```
 250    VDU 23,231,255,L1,L2,L3,L4,L5,L6,
L7
 260    VDU 23,232,Z7,Z6,Z5,Z4,Z3,Z2,Z1,2
55
 270    VDU 23,233,255,255,255,255,255,25
5,255,255
 280    M$(1)=" 9999993045000000799999999
99000 "
 290    M$(2)=" 9999993000000000079999999
95000 "
 300    M$(3)=" 9999993000000000009999517
30000 "
 310    M$(4)=" 9999950000000000007799000
30000 "
 320    M$(5)=" 7995000000000000000099000
00000 "
 330    M$(6)=" 0998003000000000000079290
00000 "
 340    M$(7)=" 0479000000000000000001192
00000 "
 350    M$(8)=" 0480000200000000000000007
02220 "
 360    M$(9)=" 0870060000000000000000000
19999 "
 370    M$(10)=" 0780690200000000000000000
004999 "
 380    M$(11)=" 0070990308220000000000000
069999 "
 390    M$(12)=" 0002200000798100000000000
049999 "
 400    M$(13)=" 0000000100000000000000000
009999 "
 410    M$(14)=" 0000000069080000000000000
004999 "
 420    M$(15)=" 0000006999890000000000000
000999 "
 430    M$(16)=" 0000069999980000000000000
000099 "
 440    COLOUR 129:COLOUR 2:PRINT:FOR J=1
 TO 16:PRINT "   ";CHR$(64+J);"  ";:FOR I
=2 TO 31:P=VAL(MID$(M$(J),I,1)):IF P=0 T
HEN PRINT " ";:GOTO 460
 450       PRINT CHR$(224+P);
 460       NEXT
 470    PRINT
 480    NEXT
 490    COLOUR 130:COLOUR 0:PRINT TAB(22,
1);".New Albion":COLOUR 129:PRINT TAB(28
,15);"Lima";:COLOUR 130:PRINT ".":COLOUR
 129:PRINT TAB(5,13);"Java":GCOL 0,3:MOV
E 160,992:DRAW 1120,992:DRAW 1120,480:DR
AW 160,480:DRAW 160,992
 500    COLOUR 129:COLOUR 3
 510    PRINT TAB(5,17);"          1
2            "
 520    PRINT TAB(5,18);"0123456789012345
67890123456789"
 530    PRINT:PRINT"Leave the Play button
 depressed"
 540    CHAIN"DRAKE2"
 550    STOP
 560    DEFPROC_TITLE
 570    COLOUR 129:COLOUR 3:CLS
 580    FORI=1TO 14:PRINT:NEXT I
 590    PRINT "     FRANCIS DRAKE":PRINT:PR
INT"     ADVENTURE GAME"
 600    FORI=1TO12:PRINT:NEXT
 610    COLOUR 2
```

```
620   PRINT"Copyright (c)":PRINT "    G.L
udinski 1983";
630   FORI=1TO3:SOUND0,-15,70,10:SOUND0
,-15,100,20:SOUND0,-10,70,20:SOUND0,-5,5
0,20:SOUND0,-2,40,20:NEXT
640   ENDPROC
```

FRANCIS DRAKE ADVENTURE GAME

```
2
    20    REM COPYRIGHT (C) G.LUDINSKI 1983
    30    DIM M$(17)
    40    COLOUR 129:COLOUR 2
    50    AL=0
    60    GOTO 130
    70    DEF FNB(N$)
    80    TF=0
    90    FOR L=0 TO 7
   100      TF=TF+(2^L)*VAL(MID$(N$,8-L,1))
   110    NEXT L
   120    =TF
   130    VDU 23,224,FNB("00010000"),FNB("0
1011010"),FNB("01011011"),FNB("01010010"
),FNB("01010111"),FNB("11111110"),FNB("0
1111110"),FNB("00111110")
   140    PROC_B
   150    SH$=CHR$(224)
   160    LA$=CHR$(136):RA$=CHR$(137):DA$=C
HR$(138):UA$=CHR$(139)
   170    M$(1)="  999999304500000079999999
99000  "
   180    M$(2)="  999999300000000079999999
95000  "
   190    M$(3)="  999999300000000009999517
30000  "
   200    M$(4)="  999995000000000007799000
30000  "
   210    M$(5)="  799500000000000000099000
00000  "
   220    M$(6)="  099800300000000000079290
00000  "
   230    M$(7)="  047900000000000000001192
00000  "
   240    M$(8)="  048000020000000000000007
02220  "
   250    M$(9)="  087006000000000000000000
19999  "
   260    M$(10)=" 078069020000000000000000
004999  "
   270    M$(11)=" 007099030822000000000000
069999  "
   280    M$(12)=" 000220000079810000000000
049999  "
   290    M$(13)=" 000000010000000000000000
009999  "
   300    M$(14)=" 000000006908000000000000
004999  "
   310    M$(15)=" 000006999890000000000000
0EEEEE  "
   320    M$(16)=" 000006999998000000000000
0EEEEE  "
   330    FOR Y=1 TO 16
   340      FOR X=2TO 31
```

```
350        C$=MID$(M$(Y),X,1)
360        IF C$="9" THEN GOTO 400
370        IF C$="0" THEN IS=INT(7*RND(1
)):PROC_ISERT:GOTO 400
380        IF C$="E" THEN IS=4:PROC_ISER
T:GOTO 400
390        IF (X > 4 AND X < 15 AND Y >
7 AND Y < 14) THEN IS=INT(2*RND(1)+7):PR
OC_ISERT ELSE IS=10:PROC_ISERT
400        NEXT:NEXT
410   CA=100:SU=100:CR=85:BA=100:DA=0:W
K=1
420   EN=0
430   X=29:Y=16:X1=29:Y1=16
440   IF WK=1 THEN COLOUR 129:COLOUR 3:
PRINT TAB(X+4,Y);SH$;CHR$(8);
450   *FX4,1
460   PRINT TAB(0,20);"Week Cargo Suppl
ies Crew Cannon Damage
            balls"
470   PRINT TAB(0,23);STRING$(39," ");
480   IF X=1 AND Y=16 THEN PRINT TAB(0,
25);"You have survived the unknown,and n
ow    know you are the first commander of
 a    fleet to sail around the world.":IF
 CA >= 400 THEN PRINT "Arise Sir Francis
":GOTO 1390
490   IF X=1 AND Y=16 THEN EN=1
500   IF (X=17 AND Y=1) OR (X=18 AND Y=
2) OR (X=19 AND Y=4) THEN AL=1
510   IF X < 15 AND AL=0 THEN PROC_B:PR
INT TAB(0,25);"Go back to New Albion"
520   IF SU <=0 THEN PROC_B:PRINT TAB(0
,25);"Your supplies have been used up so
 your crew mutinies ,and kills you":SU=0
:EN=1
530   IF CR <= 0 THEN PROC_B:PRINT TAB(
0,25);"Your crew have all been killed in
 battleor have died of scurvy,typhus or
        dysentery.You are stranded withou
t them.":CR=0:EN=1
540   IF DA > 10 THEN PROC_B:PRINT TAB(
0,25);"Your ship has filled with water a
nd sunk":EN=1
550   IF BA < 0 THEN BA=0
560   IF EN=1 THEN GOTO 1390
570   PRINT TAB(0,23);WK;TAB(6,23);CA;T
AB(12,23);SU;TAB(21,23);CR;TAB(26,23);CA
;TAB(33,23);DA
580   I$=GET$
590   PROC_B
600   IF (X=1 AND I$=LA$) OR (X=30 AND
I$=RA$) OR (Y=1 AND I$=UA$) OR (Y=16 AND
I$=DA$) THEN GOTO 580
610   IF I$=LA$ AND MID$(M$(Y),X-1,1) <
> "0" AND MID$(M$(Y),X-1,1) <> "9" AND M
ID$(M$(Y),X,1) <> "2" THEN X=X-1
620   IF I$=RA$ AND (MID$(M$(Y),X+1,1)
<> "2" ANDMID$(M$(Y),X+1,1) <> "9" AND M
ID$(M$(Y),X,1) <> "0") THEN X=X+1
630   IF I$=DA$ AND (MID$(M$(Y+1),X,1)
<> "3" AND MID$(M$(Y+1),X,1) <> "9" AND
MID$(M$(Y),X,1) <> "1") THEN Y=Y+1
640   IF I$=UA$ AND (MID$(M$(Y-1),X,1)
<> "1" AND MID$(M$(Y-1),X,1) <> "9" AND
MID$(M$(Y),X,1) <> "3") THEN Y=Y-1
650   WK=WK+1
660   IF DA <> 0 THEN DA=DA+1
```

```
670    SU=SU-1
680    PRINT TAB(X1+4,Y1);".";
690    COLOUR 3:PRINT TAB(X+4,Y);SH$;CHR
$(8);
700    IF X=X1 AND Y=Y1 AND WK <> 1 THEN
 SOUND 0,-15,53,10:PROC_REEF:GOTO 770
710    IF MID$(M$(Y),X,1)="A" AND DA <>
0 THEN DA=0:PROC_B:PRINT TAB(0,25);"You
 have arrived at a port so you can    now
 get your ship repaired":GOTO 770
720    IF MID$(M$(Y),X,1)="4" THEN PROC_
B:GOTO 770
730    IF MID$(M$(Y),X,1)="5" THEN PROC_
NAMSHIP
740    IF MID$(M$(Y),X,1)="6" THEN PROC_
SHIP
750    IF MID$(M$(Y),X,1)="7" THEN PROC_
TRADE
760    IF MID$(M$(Y),X,1)="8" THEN PROC_
HOSTILE
770    X1=X:Y1=Y
780    GOTO 460
790    DEFPROC_REEF
800    W=INT(2*RND(1))
810    IF X < 15 THEN RR$="reef" ELSE RR
$="rock"
820    PROC_B
830    IF W=0 THEN PRINT TAB(0,25);"Ther
e is a ";RR$;" ahead.Turn around":GOTO 9
00
840    PRINT TAB(0,25);"You have run agr
ound on a ";RR$;".Are you  going to thro
w cargo and guns overboard,or put out an
 anchor to windward"
850    INPUT R$:IF INSTR(R$+"          ",
"OVERBOARD") <> 0 OR INSTR(R$+"
","overboard") <> 0 THEN R$="OVERBOARD":
GOTO 880
860    IF INSTR(R$+"           ","ANCHOR") <>
 0 OR INSTR(R$+"           ","anchor") <> 0 T
HEN R$="ANCHOR":GOTO 880
870    VDU 11:GOTO 850
880    IF R$="OVERBOARD" THEN CA=CA-RND(
20):GOTO 900
890    W2=INT(2*RND(1)):PROC_B:IF W2=0 T
HEN PRINT TAB(0,25);"You have broken fre
e without any        significant damage"
 ELSE PRINT TAB(0,25);"Your ship,the Gol
den Hind,is holed.     Return to dry lan
d at once or it will    sink":DA=DA+1
900    ENDPROC
910    DEFPROC_B
920    PRINT TAB(0,25);STRING$(238," ")
930    ENDPROC
940    DEFPROC_NAMSHIP
950    PROC_B
960    IF RND(2)=1 THEN PRINT TAB(0,25);
"You see a Spanish galleon,the Cacafuego
.Are you going to attack it or ignore it
":GOTO 980
970    PRINT TAB(0,25);"You see a Spanis
h galleon,the Esprito    Santo.Are you go
ing to attack it or      ignore it"
980    INPUT R$:IF INSTR(R$+"        ","AT
TACK") <> 0 OR INSTR(R$+"         ","attack
") <> 0 THEN R$="ATTACK":GOTO 1010
990    IF INSTR(R$+"         ","IGNORE") <>
 0 OR INSTR(R$+"        ","ignore") <> 0 T
HEN R$="IGNORE":GOTO 1010
```

```
1000    VDU 11:GOTO 980
1010    IF R$="ATTACK" AND CA <= 0 THEN P
ROC_B:PRINT TAB(0,25);"You draw alongsid
e the galleon and then find you have no
 cannon balls left so   the Spanish win t
he battle and leave youto die":EN=1:GOTO
 1030
1020    IF R$="ATTACK" THEN PROC_B:PRINT
 TAB(0,25);"You fight a fierce battle and
  finally   take command of the galleon a
nd transfersits cargo to the hold of the
 Golden Hind":CA=CA+RND(20):BA=BA-RND(20)
:FORD=1TO100:NEXTD
1030    ENDPROC
1040    DEFPROC_SHIP
1050    PROC_B
1060    PRINT TAB(0,25);"You see a spanis
h galleon.Are you going to attack it or
ignore it"
1070    INPUT R$:IF INSTR(R$+"          ","AT
TACK") <> 0 OR INSTR(R$+"          ","attack
") <> 0 THEN R$="ATTACK":GOTO 1100
1080    IF INSTR(R$+"          ","IGNORE") <>
 0 OR INSTR(R$+"          ","ignore") <> 0 T
HEN R$="IGNORE":GOTO 1100
1090    VDU 11:GOTO 1070
1100    IF R$="IGNORE" THEN ENDPROC
1110    PROC_B
1120    PRINT TAB(0,25);"Are you going to
 fire your cannons at   the galleon,or s
et fire to some old    ships and let th
em drift towards it,or  sneak up alongsi
de it and board it"
1130    INPUT R$:IF INSTR(R$+"          ","CA
NNON") <> 0 OR INSTR(R$+"          ","cannon
") <> 0 THEN R$="CANNONS":GOTO 1170
1140    IF INSTR(R$+"          ","SET FIRE"
) <> 0 OR INSTR(R$+"          ","set fire"
) THEN R$="SET FIRE":GOTO 1170
1150    IF INSTR(R$+"          ","SNEAK") <> 0
 OR INSTR(R$+"          ","sneak") THEN R$="S
NEAK":GOTO 1170
1160    VDU 11:GOTO 1130
1170    PROC_B
1180    IF R$ <> "CANNONS" THEN GOTO 1210
1190    IF RND(2)=1 THEN PRINT TAB(0,25);
"Your ship gets holed and some of your
crew are shot.Return to dry land at onc
e":DA=DA+1:BA=BA-RND(20):CR=CR-RND(10):G
OTO 1210
1200    PRINT TAB(0,25);"As your ship is
smaller and lower than  the galleon,you
manage to put it out of action and board
 it,without incurring   any damage to yo
ur ship.":CA=CA+RND(20):SU=SU+RND(20):BA
=BA+RND(20)
1210    IF R$ <> "SET FIRE" THEN GOTO 125
0
1220    PROC_B
1230    IF RND(2)=1 THEN PRINT TAB(0,25);
"The wind changes direction and the
burning ships drift towards the Golden
Hind setting the mizzen mast alight.
Return to dry land at once":DA=DA+1:GOT
O 1250
1240    PRINT TAB(0,25);"The burning ship
s drift towards the    galleon setting
it alight.The captain   surrenders and y
ou transfer his cargo toyour hold":CA=CA
```

```
+RND(20):SU=SU+RND(20):BA=BA+RND(20):GOT
O 1250
 1250    IF R$ <> "SNEAK" THEN GOTO 1290
 1260    PROC_B
 1270    IF RND(2)=1 THEN PRINT TAB(0,25);
"They see you approaching and realising
 that you are English they open fire,
 shooting some of your crew and damaging
 your boat.Return to port at once":BA=BA
-RND(20):DA=DA+1:CR=CR-RND(10):GOTO1290
 1280    PRINT TAB(0,25);"They assume you
 are Spanish as English ships have never
 been this far before, so you manage to
 board the galleon and capture it and i
ts rich cargo":CA=CA+RND(20):SU=SU+RND(2
0):BA=BA+RND(20)
 1290    ENDPROC
 1300    DEFPROC_TRADE
 1310    PROC_B:PRINT TAB(0,25);"You buy c
loves cheaply from the       islanders
":CA=CA+RND(20):SU=SU+RND(20)
 1320    ENDPROC
 1330    DEFPROC_HOSTILE
 1340    PROC_B:PRINT TAB(0,25);"Hostile i
slanders pelt you with stones":CR=CR-RND
(20)
 1350    ENDPROC
 1360    DEFPROC_ISERT
 1370    IF IS <> 10 THEN M$(Y)=LEFT$(M$(Y
),X-1)+STR$(IS)+RIGHT$(M$(Y),31-X) ELSE
M$(Y)=LEFT$(M$(Y),X-1)+"A"+RIGHT$(M$(Y),
31-X)
 1380    ENDPROC
 1390    *FX4,0
 1400    END
```

NAME THE GRAPH

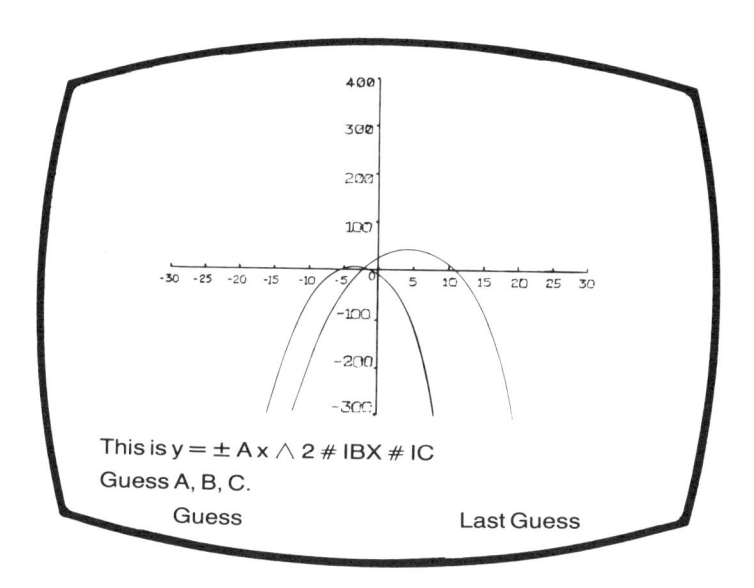

```
                    400
                    300
                    200
                    100
  -30 -25 -20 -15 -10 -5  0  5  10  15  20  25  30
                   -100
                   -200
                   -300
```

This is y = ± A x ∧ 2 # IBX # IC
Guess A, B, C.
       Guess   Last Guess

This is a game of logic. You have an aim, to find the equation of the graph that is drawn on the screen. You key in numbers to represent an equation. You can see straight away whether you are getting closer to your goal as the graph of the equation you keyed in is drawn on the screen.

By making the three numbers required larger and smaller, positive and negative, you can see how it effects the graph and hopefully, you can watch your graph getting closer and closer to the target graph until you hit it.

If you give up you will be told the answer, but don't cheat.

How to play

All graphs drawn are of the type

$$Y = Ax^2 + Bx + C$$

Where A, B and C are constants (that is numbers that can be positive or negative). For example, the equation might be

$$Y = -2x^2 + 3x - 5$$

and in this case A would be equal to -2, B equal to 3 and C to -5.

You must key in three numbers all at once on the same line and separated by commas. Press RETURN only after you have keyed in all three numbers. In the example above you would key in

-2, 3, -5 then RETURN

Then the graph of this expression is drawn and you must make another guess. If you cannot guess the answer key in

WHAT, IS, IT then RETURN

(remember to put in the commas) and you will be given the answer and the program ends.

If you guess the answer correctly then press the escape key and a new graph will be drawn.

It is more fun if you find out how to do it by trial and error, but if you want a hint to get you started then this is it. (Skip the next paragraph if you do not want to know)

If the first number (A) is positive, the graph will point upwards (u shape), and if it is negative the graph will point downwards (n shape).

Programming hints

The graphs are plotted with the origin (zero, zero point) at the middle of the screen by using the VDU statement in line 50. This saves a lot of unnecessary maths.

You could make the programs easier by reducing the range of numbers allowed. Do this by reducing the 5 in line 280 or the 9 in line 290 or both. If you wanted to make it very easy you could allow only positive numbers. To do this delete line 300.

This program is written using MODE 1 to enable the guessed graphs to be displayed in red, and the target graph in white. If you have a BBC Model A Micro then you will not have MODE 1 but if you change line 40 to MODE 4 it will work exactly the same but without colour.

```
10    REM NAME THE GRAPH
20    REM COPYRIGHT (C) G.LUDINSKI 1983
30    ON ERROR RUN
40    MODE 1:REM Put MODE 4 if you hav
e a BBC Model A Computer
50    VDU 29,640;512;
60    DEF FNY(XI)=(A**XI^2)/400+(A*D*XI)
/10+C
70    MOVE -640,0:DRAW 640,0:MOVE 0,512
:DRAW 0,-400
80    REM
90    REM DRAW AXES
100   REM
110   XA=-30:XX=0
120   FOR I=-600 TO 600 STEP 100
130      MOVE I,10:DRAW I,-10
140      PRINT TAB(XX,17);XA
150      XX=XX+3:XA=XA+5
160      IF XA=-5 THEN XX=XX+2
170   NEXT I
180   YY=25:YA=-300
190   FOR I=-300 TO 500 STEP 100
200      MOVE -10,I:DRAW 10,I
210      IF YA <> 0 THEN PRINT TAB(15,YY
);YA
220      IF YA=0 THEN YY=YY-1
230      YY=YY-3:YA=YA+100
```

```
240     NEXT I
250  REM
260  REM DRAW TARGET GRAPH
270  REM
280  A=INT(2*RND(1)+1):D=INT(5*RND(1)+2)
290  C=RND(9)
300  A=A*((-1)^RND(2)):D=D*((-1)^RND(2)):C=C*((-1)^RND(2))
310  A1=A:D1=D:C1=C:B1=2*A1*D1
320  COLOUR 3:GCOL 0,3
330  PROC_GRAPH(A,D,C)
340  REM
350  REM INPUT AND DRAW GUESSED GRAPH
360  REM
370  G=0
380  G=G+1:IF G <> 1 THEN PRINT TAB(0,1);STRING$(39," ");TAB(0,1);"Guess ";G;" Last guess = ";A$;",";B$;",";C$
390  PRINT TAB(0,28);"                                  _"
400  PRINT"This is y = +Ax^2 +Bx +C . Guess A,B,C

              ";:VDU 13:VDU 11
410  INPUT A$,B$,C$
420  IF A$="WHAT" AND B$="IS" AND C$="IT" THEN PRINT TAB(0,28);STRING$(79," ");TAB(0,29);"Answer = ";A1;",";B1;",";C1:GOTO 560
430  GCOL 0,1
440  PROC_GRAPH(VAL(A$),VAL(B$)/(2*A),VAL(C$))
450  GOTO 380
460  REM
470  DEFPROC_GRAPH(A,D,C)
480  P=0
490  COLOUR 128
500  FOR X=-600 TO 600 STEP 30
510    IF X=-600 THEN MOVE -640,FNY(-640)
520    IF FNY(X) < 650 AND FNY(X) > -450 THEN DRAW X,FNY(X):P=1
530    IF P=1 AND (FNY(X) > 650 OR FNY(X) < -450) THEN GOTO 550
540  NEXT
550  ENDPROC
560  END
```

CLOSE ENCOUNTERS OF THE FOURTH KIND

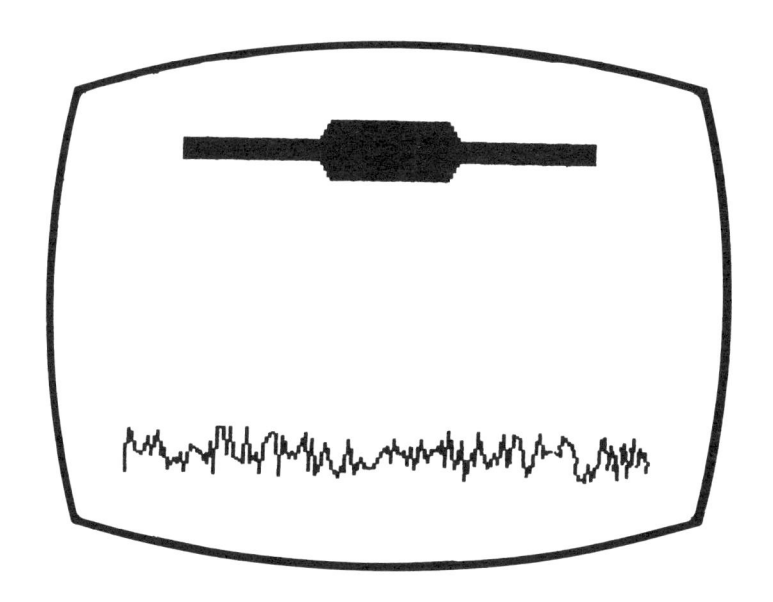

The aliens have sneaked into this book after all — but we believe they are friendly. It's up to you to find out.

Hovering above a field, lights rotating around it's outer edge, is a flying saucer. From the saucer comes a sequence of notes which may contain a message of peace. To find out you must repeat the notes in the same sequence as the aliens have transmitted them.

Every time you repeat the notes properly, the saucer will descend one level towards the ground. Try and bring them in carefully as the last time we succeeded the space vessel blew up after landing.

How to play

The number keys 0 to 9 represent a note in the octave starting with middle C.

Key in S to indicate the start of a tune.

You can either try guessing by starting with S or you can play with the keyboard until you have found the correct note.

The saucer will first emit one note and, if you copy correctly, descend slightly before sounding its next tone which will be a tune of two notes and so on. Each time you have guessed the sequence correctly the saucer will descend. Remember to start each guess with S.

If you can't find the correct note press G and RETURN and a new tune sequence will begin.

Programming hints

The sound buffer is flushed just before you key in a tune when S is pressed by using *FX15,0 in line 780. This is to prevent the last few notes the player has just keyed in from being played before the tune he is about to key in. Commands commencing with an asterisk may not be included in a line of more than one statement. I have got around this by putting *FX15,0 in a procedure and calling the procedure.

You could increase the number of possible notes in the tunes by changing the maximum value of N(L) in line 220. Then add lines for larger values of NT after line 750.

```
   10   REM CLOSE ENCOUNTERS OF THE FOURT
H KIND
   20   REM COPYRIGHT (C) G.LUDINSKI 1983
   30   MODE 5
   40   DIM N(7)
   50   CLS
   60   REM
   70   REM DRAW SPACE SHIP & GROUND
   80   REM
   90   VDU 19,2,2,0,0,0
  100   HT=964
  110   PROC_SHIP(HT,3)
  120   GCOL 0,2
  130   MOVE 0,0
  140   FOR X=0 TO 1280 STEP 10
  150     DRAW X,RND(100)
  160   NEXT X
  170   REM
  180   REM GENERATE NOTES
  190   REM
  200   FOR J=1 TO 7
  210     FOR L=1 TO J
  220       N(L)=INT(8*RND(1)+1)
  230       IF L=1 THEN GOTO 250
  240       IF N(L)=N(L-1) THEN GOTO 220
  250       PROC_PLAY(N(L))
  260     NEXT L
  270     REM
  280     REM PLAY NOTES
  290     REM
  300     EI=0
  310     I=140
  320     FOR K=1 TO J
  330       I$=INKEY$(0):IF I$ <> "G" AND
 I$ <> "S" AND (I$="" OR I$ < "1" OR I$
 > "9") THEN I=I+50:PROC_LIGHTS(HT):GOTO
 330
  340       IF I$="G" THEN K=J:GOTO 380
  350       IF I$="S" THEN PROC_FLUSH:K=1
:GOTO 330
  360       PROC_PLAY(VAL(I$))
  370       IF VAL(I$) <> N(K) THEN EI=1
  380     NEXT K
  390     IF I$="G" THEN GOTO 210
  400     IF EI=0 THEN PROC_SHIP(HT,0):HT
=HT-120:PROC_SHIP(HT,3):PROC_ROTATE:GOTO
 420
  410     GOTO 300
  420   NEXT J
  430   REM
  440   REM EXPLOSION
  450   REM
  460   FOR I=1 TO 100:VDU 19,0,1,0,0,0,1
9,0,3,0,0,0:NEXT I:GOTO 840
  470   REM
  480   DEFPROC_SHIP(HT,CL)
  490   GCOL 0,CL
  500   PROC_BLOCK(140,HT-20,1000,40)
  510   MOVE 460,HT
  520   MOVE 500,HT-60:PLOT 85,500,HT+60
  530   MOVE 820,HT
  540   MOVE 780,HT-60:PLOT 85,780,HT+60
  550   PROC_BLOCK(500,HT-60,280,120)
  560   ENDPROC
  570   DEFPROC_BLOCK(X,Y,W,H)
  580   MOVE X,Y:MOVE X+W,Y
  590   PLOT 85,X,Y+H
  600   PLOT 85,X+W,Y+H
  610   ENDPROC
```

```
 520    DEFPROC_LIGHTS(HT)
 530    IF I >= 1090THEN GCOL 0,3:PROC_BL
OCK(I,HT-20,50,40):I=140
 640    GCOL 0,3:PROC_BLOCK(I,HT-20,50,40
)
 650    GCOL 0,1:PROC_BLOCK(I+50,HT-20,50
,40)
 660    ENDPROC
 670    DEFPROC_PLAY(NT)
 680    IF NT=1 THEN SOUND 1,-15,53,10
 690    IF NT=2 THEN SOUND 1,-15,61,10
 700    IF NT=3 THEN SOUND 1,-15,69,10
 710    IF NT=4 THEN SOUND 1,-15,73,10
 720    IF NT=5 THEN SOUND 1,-15,81,10
 730    IF NT=6 THEN SOUND 1,-15,89,10
 740    IF NT=7 THEN SOUND 1,-15,97,10
 750    IF NT=8 THEN SOUND 1,-15,101,10
 760    ENDPROC
 770    DEFPROC_ROTATE
 780    *FX15,0
 790    FOR D=1 TO 50:I=I+50:PROC_LIGHTS(
HT):NEXT D
 800    ENDPROC
 810    DEFPROC_FLUSH
 820    *FX15,0
 830    ENDPROC
 840    REM
```

SEQUENCE COUNTDOWN

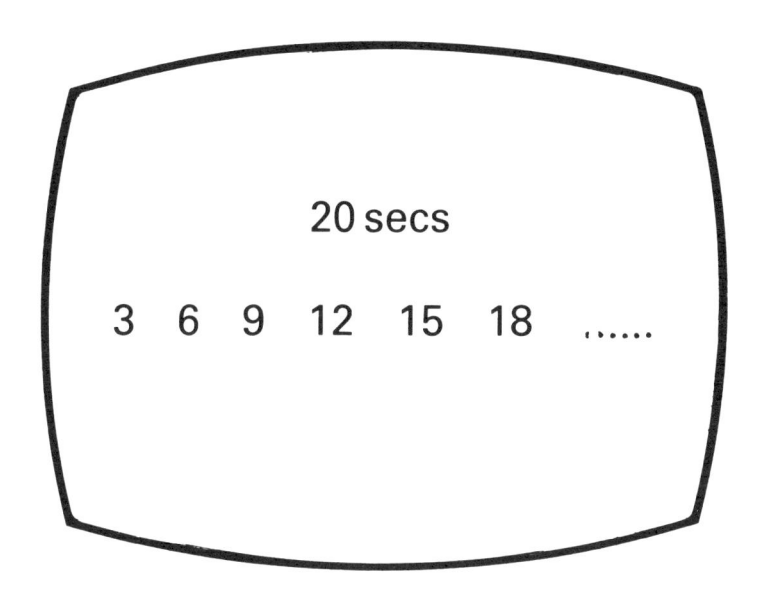

```
           20 secs

    3  6  9  12  15  18  ......
```

Six numbers, or letters, will be displayed on the screen and it is up to you to provide the next logical item to complete the series.

How to play

When you have worked out your answer, type in your item and press RETURN.

If you cannot work out the correct answer, then move on as quickly as possible as you only have 200 seconds to complete as many answers as you can.

A wrong answer will bring you the correct result from your computer, and then you will be handed back to the next sequence. If you wish to PASS on a question then press P and RETURN and you will be taken on to the next question.

After 200 seconds your score sheet will be displayed showing the number of sequences tried, correct answers, your time, and your IQ level for adaptibility.

Programming hints

This program has a useful facility that enables the time to be constantly displayed in seconds. This actually only occurs while the program is waiting for the player to key in something, but as most of any program's time is taken up with waiting, this is all that is required. The lines 330 and 340 perform this function. In line 330 the time is printed out until the first character is keyed in. Then in line 340 subsequent characters are accepted until the Return key is pressed. The Return key has an ASCII value of 13, so is represented by CHR$(13).

One change you couuld make, is to add new sequences. To do this allow W to have a larger maximum value in line 170. The sequence must then be defined after line 210. The sequence is held in S(2), S(3), S(4), S(5), S(6), S(7) and S(8). S(2) is defined in line 150 and is fixed for all sequences. IC is another random value which may be useful when defining a sequence. The message saying how the sequence is created is held in MS$. If the last number in sequence S(8) is less than 26 then the sequence is converted to letters.

```
10    REM SEQUENCE COUNTDOWN
20    REM COPYRIGHT (C) G.LUDINSKI 1983
30    MODE 4
40    DIM S(8),IP$(255)
50    CLS
```

```
60    VDU 23,224,0,1,2,4,136,80,32,0
70    TE=0:CR=0:TIME=0
80    CLS
90    TE=TE+1
100   IF TE=11 OR TIME >= 20000 THEN GO
TO 510
110   REM
120   REM WORK OUT SEQUENCE
130   REM
140   S(1)=0
150   S(2)=INT(RND(1)*9+1)
160   IC=INT(RND(1)*9+1)
170   W=INT(RND(1)*3)
180   FOR I=3 TO 8
190      IF W=0 THEN S(I)=2*S(I-1)-S(I-2
)+IC:MS$="The interval increases by "+ST
R$(IC)+" each time"
200      IF W=1 THEN S(I)=S(I-1)+S(I-2)+
IC:MS$="Each number is the sum of the pr
evious two plus "+STR$(IC)
210      IF W=2 THEN S(I)=S(2)^(I-1):MS$
="Each number is "+STR$(S(2))+" to the p
ower of 1,2,3,4,5,6 and 7"
220      NEXT I
230   FOR I=1 TO 13:PRINT:NEXT I
240   REM
250   REM DISPLAY SEQUENCE
260   REM
270   IF S(8) > 26 THEN PRINT STR$(S(2)
);" ";STR$(S(3));" ";STR$(S(4));" ";STR$
(S(5));" ";STR$(S(6));" ";STR$(S(7));"
......";:LE=0
280   IF S(8) <= 26 THEN LE=1:PRINT CHR
$(64+S(2));" ";CHR$(64+S(3));" ";CHR$(64
+S(4));" ";CHR$(64+S(5));" ";CHR$(64+S(6
));" ";CHR$(64+S(7));"  ......";
290   REM
300   REM INPUT ANSWER
310   REM
320   IX=1
330   IP$(IX)=INKEY$(10):IF IP$(IX)=""
THEN PRINT TAB(0,1);INT(TIME/100):GOTO 3
30
340   PRINT TAB(IX,15);IP$(IX);:IX=IX+1
:IP$(IX)=GET$:IF IP$(IX) <> CHR$(13) THE
N GOTO 340
350   I$="":FOR I=1 TO IX-1:I$=I$+IP$(I
):NEXT I
360   REM
370   REM CHECK ANSWER
380   REM
390   *FX 15,1
400   IF LE=0 AND ABS(VAL(I$) - S(8))
<= LEN(I$)/2 THEN COLOUR1:PRINT" ";CHR$(
224):CR=CR+1:COLOUR 3:GOTO 450
410   IF LE=1 AND (I$=CHR$(64+S(8)) OR
I$=CHR$(65+S(8))) THEN COLOUR1:PRINT" "
;CHR$(224):CR=CR+1:COLOUR 3:GOTO 450
420   PRINT:PRINT:PRINT"No, the answer =
";S(8)
430   IF LE=1 THEN PRINT:PRINT"Replace
each letter by its position      number e
.9. 1 for A,2 for B etc."
440   PRINT:PRINT MS$
450   PRINT:PRINT"Press Return to conti
nue"
460   INPUT A$
470   GOTO 80
480   REM
```

```
490  REM SCORE SHEET
500  REM
510  CLS:PRINT
520  PRINT"Number of sequences complet
ed = ";TE
530  PRINT:PRINT"Number correct = ";CR
540  PRINT:PRINT"Time taken = ";INT(TI
ME/100);" seconds"
550  IQ=INT(CR*100/5.3)
560  PRINT:PRINT"Your IQ level (adapta
bility) = ";IQ
570  PRINT
580  IF CR >= 7 THEN PRINT"This is cla
ssed as SUPERIOR (upper 10%)":GOTO 610
590  IF CR = 6 THEN PRINT"This is clas
sed as GOOD (upper 20%)":GOTO 610
600  IF CR = 5 THEN PRINT"This is clas
sed as FAIR (upper 60%)"
610  REM
```

SPIRAL MAZES

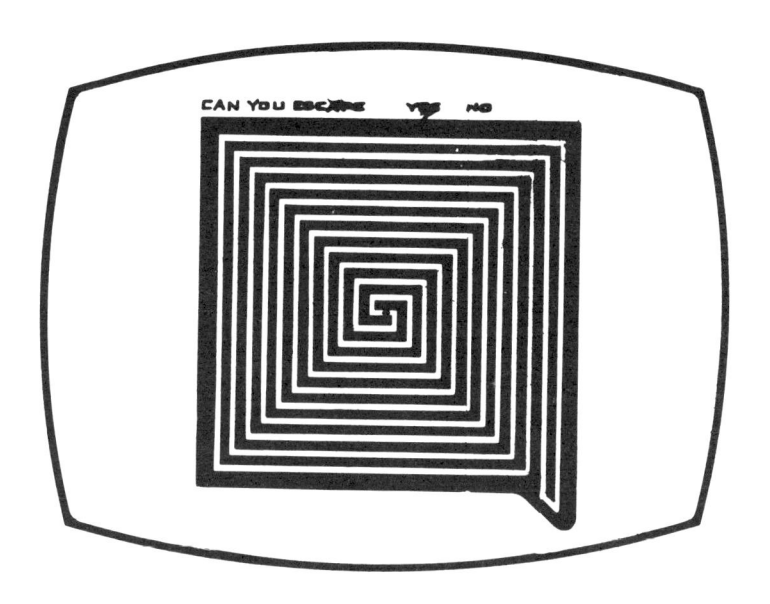

Because you forgot to doff your cap to the local tyrant, you have been thrown into his dungeons.

On the floor, scratched by a previous resident, is a map so now is your chance to escape. Rather than rush head-long into the maze, however, it would be wise to trace your way through in advance. Try drawing a continuous line from where you are to the outside of the dungeons.

By the way, if you make it to the outside, don't forget about doffing the cap next time.

How to play

A maze will be drawn on the screen. At first glance it may

appear to be a simple spiral but it may be an optical illusion.

Your position, at the centre, is marked by a red line and you move by pressing the ARROW keys.

Like Dorothy, in the Wizard of Oz, your path will be shown as a yellow line.

When you have decided whether or not your escape is possible press Y for Yes and N for No.

Programming hints

If you wish to change the direction in which the spiral is wound, then you may change the initial values of XS and YS.

If you wish to make the end wall, which blocks off the outside of the maze, run at right angles, then you should change line 320 from PLOT 1, XC, YC to two alternative lines.

          PLOT 1, O, YC: PLOT 1, XC, O
and   PLOT 1, XC, O: PLOT 1, O, YC

You will have to remember to separate the conditions in lines 280 to 310 to determine in which order the PLOT statements occur.

```
10    REM SPIRAL MAZE
20    REM COPYRIGHT (C) G.LUDINSKI 1983
30    MODE 5
40    CLS
50    WH=INT(RND(1)*2)
60    PA=(2*INT(RND(1)*8))+8
70    L=30:W=30:X=600:Y=470
80    REM
90    REM DRAW MAZE
100   REM
110   FOR J=1 TO 2
120      XS=1:YS=-1
130      GCOL 0,1:MOVE X-15,Y-15:PLOT 1,
```

```
30,0:GCOL 0,3
  140      IF J=1 THEN MOVE X,Y:SP=-1:XT=X
:YT=Y
  150      IF J=2 THEN MOVE X,Y:PLOT 1,-W,
0:PLOT 1,0,W:SP=1
  160      FOR I=1 TO PA
  170          IF WH=1 AND J=2 AND I >= (PA-
3) THEN I=PA:GOTO 220
  180          IF I/2 = INT(I/2) THEN YP=YS*
(L+(2*INT((I+SP)/2))*W): PLOT 1,0,YP:YS=
-YS
  190          IF I/2 = INT(I/2) AND J=1 TH
EN YT=YT+YP
  200          IF I/2 <> INT(I/2) THEN XP=(L
+(2*INT((I+SP)/2))*W)*XS:PLOT 1,XP,0:XS=
-XS
  210          IF I/2 <> INT(I/2) AND J=1 T
HEN XT=XT+XP
  220      NEXT I
  230    NEXT J
  240  REM
  250  REM BLOCK OFF END OF MAZE
  260  REM
  270  XC=0:YC=0
  280  IF (WH=0 AND XT > X) OR (WH=1 AND
 XT < X) THEN XC=-W
  290  IF (WH=0 AND XT < X) OR (WH=1 AND
 XT > X) THEN XC=W
  300  IF (WH=0 AND YT > Y) OR (WH=1 AND
 YT < Y) THEN YC=-W
  310  IF (WH=0 AND YT < Y) OR (WH=1 AND
 YT > Y) THEN YC=W
  320  PLOT 1,XC,YC
  330  PRINT TAB(0,1);"Can you escape (Y
/N)"
  340  REM
  350  REM DRAW PATH THROUGH MAZE
  360  REM
  370  PROC_ARROW
  380  REM
  390  REM CHECK ANSWER
  400  REM
  410  PRINTTU$
  420  IF ( TU$="Y" AND WH=0) OR (TU$="N
" AND WH=1) THEN PRINT"You are right":GO
TO 440
  430  PRINT"You are wrong"
  440  *FX4,0
  450  GOTO 780
  460  REM
  470  DEFPROC_ARROW
  480  MOVE X-20,Y-15
  490  GCOL 0,2
  500  *FX4,1
  510  TU$=GET$
  520  IF TU$="Y" OR TU$="N" THEN GOTO 6
10
  530  X0=0:Y0=0
  540  IF TU$ < CHR$(136) OR TU$ > CHR$(
139) THEN GOTO 510
  550  IF TU$=CHR$(136) THEN X0=-5
  560  IF TU$=CHR$(137) THEN X0=5
  570  IF TU$=CHR$(138) THEN Y0=-5
  580  IF TU$=CHR$(139) THEN Y0=5
  590  PLOT 1,X0,Y0
  600  GOTO 510
  610  GCOL 0,3
  620  ENDPROC
  780  REM
```

WHAT'S YOURS

Do you know that awful feeling when you have been put in charge of the drinks purchase at your friend's wedding?

You can be sure that you will get a soft drink for the big fellow in the corner or, even worse, a double whisky with pint chaser for someone's grandmother.

Anyway, it's your turn to buy the drinks and the order is on the bar. If you remember to get everyone the correct drink you will receive a whisky from each of them as they will be so pleased with your effort. If you get the **total** round correct, they will all pitch in and pay for the drinks themselves.

All the drinks are £1 each, so everytime you get the round right you make £1 per drink for yourself.

Oh, we almost forgot, everytime you get it right someone else joins your circle of friends.

How to play

Five different types of drinks can be ordered as follows:-

Beer	Red Mug	B
Lager	Yellow Mug	L
Red Wine	Red Glass	R
White Wine	White Glass	W
Whisky	Yellow Glass	—

Look at the order detail on the bar and key in your copy. As you key in your order, the drinks will appear on the screen. When you finish the first round, a second will appear in a different order and, if the last round was correct, an additional member will be added to your group.

When the drink runs out, you can go home — by taxi.

Programming hints

This program is a good example of the use of user-defined graphics. Just two shapes are defined, a glass and a mug shape, but as they are displayed in many different colours there appears to be a large number of shapes. Remember to use COLOUR and not GCOL for user-defined graphics, as they are handled in the same way as text.

You may wish to add some more drinks in the appropriate shaped glass or mug. For example, a white beer mug could represent lemonade, or you could define a brandy or sherry glass shape. If you add more drinks you must allow W in line 320 to have a larger maximum value. Check for the letter that represents the new drinks in line 480. Display the new drinks after line 520.

```
10    REM WHAT'S YOURS
20    REM COPYRIGHT (C) G.LUDINSKI 1983
30    MODE 5
40    DIM W(20)
50    GOTO 150
60    DEF FNB(N$)
70    TF=0
80    FOR L=0 TO 7
90      TF=TF+(2^L)*VAL(MID$(N$,8-L,1))
100   NEXT L
110   =TF
120   REM
130   REM DEFINE GLASS AND BEER MUG SHAPE
140   REM
150   VDU 23,224,FNB("00111110"),FNB("00111110"),FNB("00111110"),FNB("00011100"),FNB("00001000"),FNB("00001000"),FNB("00001000"),FNB("00111110")
160   VDU 23,225,FNB("01111000"),FNB("01111000"),FNB("01111110"),FNB("01111010"),FNB("01111010"),FNB("01111010"),FNB("01111010"),FNB("01111000")
170   MG$=CHR$(225):GL$=CHR$(224)
180   REM
190   REM DRAW BAR AND NOTE PADS
200   REM
210   CLS
220   GCOL 0,1:PROC_BLOCK(0,520,1279,240)
230   GCOL 0,3:PROC_BLOCK(250,0,255,280)
240   GCOL 0,3:PROC_BLOCK(755,0,270,280)
250   COLOUR 0:COLOUR 131:PRINT TAB(4,24);"Bill":PRINT TAB(12,24);"Back":PRINT TAB(4,26);"`":PRINT TAB(12,26);"`":COLOUR 3:COLOUR 128
260   REM
270   REM DRAW DRINKS ORDERED
280   REM
290   M=0:OW=0
300   FOR J=2 TO 20
310     FOR I=1 TO J
320       W(I)=INT(RND(1)*4)
330       IF W(I)=0 THEN CL=1:C$=GL$
340       IF W(I)=1 THEN CL=1:C$=MG$
350       IF W(I)=2 THEN CL=2:C$=MG$
360       IF W(I)=3 THEN CL=3:C$=GL$
370       COLOUR CL:PRINT TAB(I-1,7);C$;:PRINT TAB(I-1,16);" ";
380     NEXT I
390     EI=0
```

```
 400      COLOUR 3:COLOUR 128:PRINT TAB(0
,18);"What is your order   B=beer   L=Lage
r     R=red & W=white wine"
 410      OW=OW+J
 420      REM
 430      REM DRAW DRINKS BOUGHT
 440      REM
 450      FOR K=1 TO J
 460        I$=GET$
 470        IF K=1 THEN PRINT TAB(0,7);ST
RING$(20," ");
 480        IF I$ <> "B" AND I$ <> "L" AN
D I$ <> "R" AND I$ <> "W" THEN GOTO 460
 490        IF I$="R" THEN COLOUR 1:PRINT
 TAB(K-1,7);GL$:IP=0
 500        IF I$="W" THEN COLOUR 3:PRINT
 TAB(K-1,7);GL$:IP=3
 510        IF I$="B" THEN COLOUR 1:PRINT
 TAB(K-1,7);MG$:IP=1
 520        IF I$="L" THEN COLOUR 2:PRINT
 TAB(K-1,7);MG$:IP=2
 530        IF IP=W(K) THEN COLOUR 2:PRIN
T TAB(K-1,16);GL$;:M=M+1:GOTO 550
 540        EI=1
 550        COLOUR 0:COLOUR 131:PRINT TAB
(5,26);OW:PRINT TAB(13,26);M:COLOUR 128
 560      NEXT K
 570      IF EI=0 THEN M=M+J:COLOUR 0:COL
OUR 131:PRINT TAB(13,26);M:COLOUR 128
 580      RB$=INKEY$(50*J)
 590      *FX 15,1
 600      IF EI=1 THEN GOTO 310
 610    NEXT J
 620    PRINT TAB(0,16);"You did it ! you
    will need a real     drink after that
    ";
 630    REM
 640    DEFPROC_BLOCK(X,Y,W,H)
 650    MOVE X,Y:MOVE X+W,Y
 660    PLOT 85,X,Y+H
 670    PLOT 85,X+W,Y+H
 680    ENDPROC
```

PATTERN PAIRS

If you have tried Odd One Out in this book, then you will find this following puzzle a little more difficult.

There are nine patterns displayed on the screen, in a range of colours, and you have only a few seconds to compare them and nominate the pair, you believe, are a match.

How to play

Identify your pair, note the numbers alongside and key in your answer. You don't have to key in your answer in strict chronological order. Just punch in your numbers and wait. Correct responses will be rewarded with a pleasant little high pitched tune, but wrong answers will be faced with a low pitched little dirge.

To continue, press Y for Yes and to stop, press N for No, remembering to press RETURN after your response.

A score sheet will appear at the end showing your tries, results, time and average time.

Programming hints

Each of the patterns is slightly different except for the matching pair. This is done by adding a mixture of H1, H2 and H3 to the corners of the triangles in procedure PROC_PATTERN and H1, H2 and H3 will be different for each pattern except the two that are the same.

If you wish to increase the number of patterns which are the same, then a W3 should be assigned. W3 should be a random number between 1 and 9 inclusive and you should check that it is not equal to W1 or W2. Then change W$ and W1$ and assign four more values, say, W2$, W3$, W4$ and W5$ with the string of W1, W2 and W3 arranged in all possible different ways.

Then check for PT to be equal to W1, W2 or W3 in line 720 in procedure PROC_PATTERN to see whether the pattern to be drawn is one of the three identical ones.

Change the input lines 440 to 510 to allow a third number to be keyed in and then check for the six possible values W$, W1$ to W5$.

```
10   REM PATTERN PAIRS
20   REM COPYRIGHT (C) G.LUDINSKI 1983
30   DIM X(4,3),Y(4,3),C(4)
40   MODE 5
50   NU=0:CR=0
60   TIME=0
70   CLS
80   NU=NU+1
90   PT=0:PC=0
```

```
100 REM
110 REM DRAW FRAMEWORK
120 REM
130 GCOL 0,2:COLOUR 3
140 MOVE 426,255:DRAW 426,1023
150 MOVE 852,255:DRAW 852,1023
160 MOVE 0,255:DRAW 1279,255
170 MOVE 0,510:DRAW 1279,510
180 MOVE 0,765:DRAW 1279,765
190 REM
200 REM GENERATE SHAPES
210 REM
220 W1=RND(9)
230 W2=RND(9):IF W2=W1 THEN GOTO 230
240 W$=STR$(W1)+STR$(W2)
250 W1$=STR$(W2)+STR$(W1)
260 FOR I=1 TO 4
270    C(I)=INT(RND(1)*3+1)
280    FOR J=1 TO 3
290       X(I,J)=INT(RND(1)*320+30)
300       Y(I,J)=INT(RND(1)*160+30)
310    NEXT J
320 NEXT I
330 REM
340 REM DRAW PATTERNS
350 REM
360 FOR J=765 TO 255 STEP -255
370    FOR I=0 TO 852 STEP 426
380       PROC_PATTERN(I,J)
390    NEXT I
400 NEXT J
410 REM
420 REM QUESTION
430 REM
440 PRINT TAB(0,25),"Which 2 are the same",
450 I$="":I=0:IC=0
460 I1$=INKEY$(0):IF I1$ = "" OR I1$ < "1" OR I1$ > "9" THEN GOTO 460
470 PRINT I1$,
480 IF IC=0 THEN IC=IC+1:I$=I$+I1$:GOTO 460
490 I$=I$+I1$
510 IF I$=W$ OR I$=W1$ THEN PRINT:PRINT"Yes,you are right":SOUND 1,-15,101,30:CR=CR+1:GOTO 530
520 PRINT:PRINT"No, ",LEFT$(W$,1),," and ",RIGHT$(W$,1),," are the same":SOUND 1,-15,73,10:SOUND 1,-15,69,5
530 PRINT:PRINT"Do you want more Y/N",
540 INPUT R$
550 IF R$ <> "N" THEN GOTO 70
560 REM
570 REM SCORE SHEET
580 REM
590 CLS
600 PRINT:PRINT"      Pattern Pairs"
610 FOR I=1 TO 9:PRINT:NEXT I
620 PRINT:PRINT"Problems completed =",NU
630 TM=INT(TIME/100)
640 PRINT:PRINT"Problems correct = ",CR
650 PRINT:PRINT"Time taken = ",TM:PRINT"secs"
660 IF CR <> 0 THEN PRINT:PRINT"Time / Problem = ",INT(TM/CR):PRINT"secs"
```

```
  670    GOTO 810
  680    REM
  690    DEFPROC_PATTERN(XD,YD)
  700    PT=PT+1
  710    PRINT TAB(((20*XD)/1279)+1,31-(32
*YD)/1023),PT
  720    IF PT=VAL(RIGHT$(W$,1)) OR PT=VAL
(LEFT$(W$,1)) THEN H1=80:H2=80:H3=80:GOT
O 740
  730    PC=PC+1:H1=PC*10:H2=PC*10:H3=PC*1
0
  740    FOR L=1 TO 4
  742      CL=RND(3):IF PT=VAL(RIGHT$(W$,1
)) OR PT=VAL(LEFT$(W$,1)) THEN CL=C(L)
  750      GCOL 0,CL
  760      MOVE (X(L,1)+XD+H1),(Y(L,1)+YD+
H1)
  770      MOVE (X(L,2)+XD+H2),(Y(L,2)+YD+
H1)
  780      PLOT 85,(X(L,3)+XD+H3),(Y(L,3)+
YD-INT(H1/2))
  790    NEXT L
  800    ENDPROC
  810    REM END
```

CONCENTRATION TEST

This time we have given a little longer to work out your answers, because we think you'll need all the brainpower at your command.

On the screen will be displayed 23 rows of 35 numbers and you have 'eight' minutes to find as many pairs of adjacent numbers, whose sum is 10, as possible.

These pairs must be in the same row.

How to play

When you have found the matching pairs, key in the row number followed by the column number of each, and then press RETURN Example A3, A4. Always place a comma between each entry. If your pair of numbers is correct they will be displayed in different colours to the surrounding numbers (i.e. reversed)

You may key in the pairs in any order and, if you cannot find any 'missing' pairs before your time is up, type in NO, MORE followed by RETURN. Again, there must be a comma between the words.

This ending of the game will cause your score sheet to be displayed. If you fail to complete in the alloted time the score sheet will automatically appear.

Your score sheet will give a classification and an IQ rating on your powers of concentration.

Programming hints

Lines 100-230 draw out the matrix of numbers and the row and column labels. Note that the letters are displayed in a loop by referring to their ASCII values. As the letter A has ASCII value of 65, B has a value of 66 etc so CHR$(64+J) where J is 1,2,3 etc. will display the letters A,B,C etc.

I would not advise any alterations as the scoring and IQ levels were determined by scientific testing, and any changes would make the scores and IQ level incorrect.

```
10    REM CONCENTRATION TESTER
20    REM COPYRIGHT (C) G.LUDINSKI 1983
30    *KEY 10 "OLD!M"
40    MODE 4
50    DIM A$(35,23)
60    CLS
70    NU=0
80    TIME=0
90    ER=0
100   REM
110   REM DRAW MATRIX
120   REM
130   PRINT
140   PRINT"               1              2
   3"
150   PRINT"   12345678901234567890123456789012345
6789012345"
```

```
160    FOR J=1 TO 23
170      PRINT:PRINTCHR$(64+J);" ";
180      FOR I=1 TO 35
190        A$(I,J)=STR$(INT(RND(1)*10))
200        PRINTA$(I,J);
210        NEXT I
220      PRINT " ";CHR$(64+J);
230    NEXT J
240  REM
250  REM QUESTION
260  REM
270  PRINT
280  PRINT TAB(0,28);"Type row col. co
mma row col. so X+Y=10   ";
290  PRINT:INPUT C$,D$
300  REM
310  REM CHECK INPUT
320  REM
330  IF TIME >= 48000 THEN GOTO 490
340  IF C$="NO" AND D$="MORE" THEN GOT
O 490
350  IF LEN(C$) < 2 OR LEN(D$) < 2 THE
N PROC_ERROR:GOTO 290
360  J=ASC(LEFT$(C$,1))-64
370  I=VAL(MID$(C$,2,LEN(C$)-1))
380  K=ASC(LEFT$(D$,1))-64
390  L=VAL(MID$(D$,2,LEN(D$)-1))
400  IF I < 1 OR I > 35 OR J < 1 OR J
 > 23 OR L < 1 OR L > 35 OR K < 1 OR K >
 23 THEN PROC_ERROR:GOTO 290
410  IF J <> K THEN PROC_ERROR:GOTO 29
0
420  IF VAL(A$(I,J))+VAL(A$(L,K)) <> 1
0 THEN ER=ER+1:PROC_ERROR:GOTO 290
430  COLOUR 129:COLOUR 0:PRINTTAB(I+1,
J+3);A$(I,J);:PRINTTAB(L+1,K+3);A$(L,K);
:COLOUR 128:COLOUR 1
440  NU=NU+1
450  PRINT TAB(0,30);"              ":VDU 11
:VDU 11:VDU 11:VDU 11:GOTO 280
460  REM
470  REM SCORE SHEET
480  REM
490  CLS:PRINT:PRINT:PRINT"You found "
;NU;" pairs"
500  MAX=0
510  FOR J=1 TO 23
520    FOR I=1 TO 34
530      IF VAL(A$(I,J))+VAL(A$(I+1,J)
)=10 THEN MAX=MAX+1
540    NEXT I
550  NEXT J
560  SCORE=MAX-NU+ER
570  PRINT:PRINT"Your score is ";SCORE
:PRINT
580  AV=MAX * 0.6:IQ = INT((NU / AV) *
100)
590  IF IQ > 150 THEN IQ=150
600  IF SCORE < 0.6*SCORE THEN PRINT"Y
ou are classed as SUPERIOR (upper 10%)":
GOTO 640
610  IF SCORE < 0.9*SCORE THEN PRINT"Y
ou are classed as GOOD (upper 30%)":GOTO
 640
620  IF SCORE < 1.1*SCORE THEN PRINT"Y
ou are classed as FAIR (upper 60%)"
640  PRINT:PRINT"Your IQ level (concen
tration) = ";IQ
```

```
650    PRINT:PRINT"Do you want more (Y/N
)"
660    INPUT I$
670    IF I$ <> "Y" AND I$ <> "N" THEN V
DU 11:GOTO 660
680    IF I$="Y" THEN GOTO 60
690    GOTO 740
700    REM
710    DEFPROC_ERROR
720    VDU 11:VDU 11:VDU 11:PRINT"Error:
type row,col. comma row col.so =10";
730    ENDPROC
740    REM END
```

WIRE MAZE

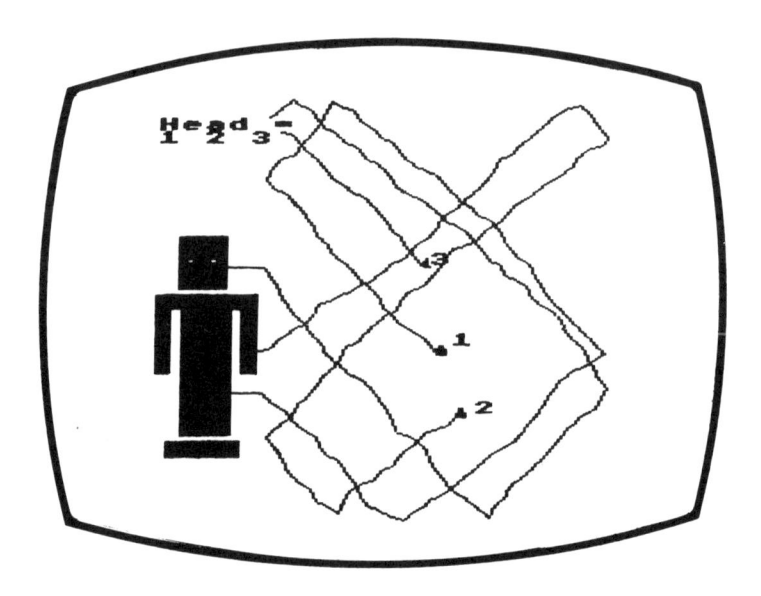

Well at last you have your own robot to cut the grass, clean the car, wash the windows and take the dog for a walk. There is one snag, however.

Your robot has been wired up incorrectly. It must have been Friday afternoon when the other robots put your model together. At the moment, if you press the arm-control button the robot's legs move. You, I'm afraid, are going to have to rewire your new family friend.

How to play

As the program begins, your robot will be drawn on the screen. When the robot shape is completed, the screen will go black and the wiring will be added along with the control buttons. The robot, complete with wires and buttons will reappear and you will then have to trace the wiring.

Control buttons are:

> Red   1
> Yellow 2
> White 3

At the top of the screen will appear the word Head and the three colour buttons. You must decide which of these buttons is connected to the head and press the corresponding number key and RETURN. One wrong try means you must try again, and a subsequent wrong guess will cause your computer to give you the correct answer. If you think about it, if you have guessed two wrong from three, you should know the answer by now anyway.

You continue for the arms, legs.

To play again, with a different maze, press RUN.

Programming hints

The useful BLOCK procedure is used which draws a rectangle of a specified size at a specified place. The rectangle is created by drawing TWO right-angled triangles joined together. Each triangle is drawn by MOVEing to a point then drawing a line by moving to another point and then drawing a line from this point to a third point. If PLOT 85 is used to draw this line from the second point then a filled-in triangle is created. You could use this procedure in any of your own non-commercial programs. Copy in the procedure DEF PROC_BLOCK (X,Y,W,H) and call it with PROC_BLOCK (followed by the

X and Y position of its bottom left hand corner followed by its width and height all separated by commas.

The other thing about the program that you might find useful, is the way it draws the maze without you seeing it. This is done by using the VDU 19 command to change all red (1), yellow (2) and white (3) pictures to black (0). The maze is then drawn. Then another set of VDU 19 commands changes them all back to their original colours. The colour numbers are not the same as the second number is the logical colour number; the colour numbering system that is applicable to all modes.

You might find the wire maze too easy. It can be made more difficult by increasing the length of each wire by increasing the larger number in line 420.

```
 10 REM WIRE MAZE
 20 REM COPYRIGHT (C) G.LUDINSKI 1983
 30 DIM XA(3)
 40 DIM YA(3)
 50 DIM W(3)
 60 *KEY 10 "OLD!M"
 70 MODE 5
 80 CLS
 90 REM
100 REM DRAW ROBOT
110 REM
120 GCOL 0,2
130 PROC_BLOCK(70,550,125,125)
140 GCOL 0,3:PROC_BLOCK(0,500,275,35)
150 PROC_BLOCK(0,350,35,150)
160 PROC_BLOCK(240,350,39,150)
170 PROC_BLOCK(75,350,125,150)
180 GCOL 0,2:PROC_BLOCK(75,200,125,15
0)
190 PROC_BLOCK(35,150,200,35)
200 COLOUR 0:COLOUR 130:PRINTTAB(1,12
),".."; COLOUR 2:COLOUR 128
210 REM
220 REM DECIDE WHICH CONTROLS CONNECT
 TO WHICH PARTS
230 REM
240 FOR I = 1 TO 3
250    W(I)=INT(RND(1)*3+1)
260    IF (I=2 AND W(I)=W(1)) OR (I=3
 AND (W(I)=W(2) OR W(I)=W(1))) THEN GOTO
 250
270 NEXT I
280 REM
290 REM DRAW WIRES
300 REM
310    GCOL 0,2
320 XA(1)=300:YA(1)=600:MOVE 200,600:
```

```
              DRAW XA(1),YA(1)
       330    XA(2)=300:YA(2)=400:MOVE 275,400:
DRAW XA(2),YA(2)
       340    XA(3)=300:YA(3)=300:MOVE 200,300:
DRAW XA(3),YA(3)
       350    VDU 30
       360    VDU 19,1,0,0,0,0
       370    VDU 19,2,0,0,0,0
       380    VDU 19,3,0,0,0,0
       390    FOR I=1 TO 3
       400      XS=(-1)^I:YS=(-1)^I
       410      MOVE XA(I),YA(I)
       420      FOR J = 1 TO 100
       430        DX=XS*INT(RND(1)*30+10)
       440        IF ((XA(I)+DX) < 300 OR (XA(I
)+DX) > 1278) THEN XS=-XS:GOTO 430
       450        XA(I)=XA(I)+DX
       460        DY=YS*INT(RND(1)*20+10)
       470        IF ((YA(I)+DY) < 0 OR (YA(I)+
DY) > 1020) THEN YS=-YS:GOTO 460
       480        YA(I)=YA(I)+DY
       490        DRAW XA(I),YA(I)
       500      NEXT J
       510    REM
       520    REM DRAW BUTTONS
       530    REM
       540      GCOL 0,W(I):PROC_BLOCK(XA(I),YA
(I),20,10):PROC_BLOCK(XA(I)+5,YA(I)+10,1
0,10):GCOL 0,2
       550      PRINT TAB(INT(XA(I)/64)+1,INT((
1023-YA(I))/32)-1);W(I);
       560    NEXT I
       570   REM
       580   REM TURN DISPLAY BACK ON
       590   REM
       600   VDU 19,1,1,0,0,0
       610   VDU 19,2,3,0,0,0
       620   VDU 19,3,7,0,0,0
       630   REM
       640   REM WRITE QUESTIONS
       650   REM
       660   FOR I=1 TO 3:PROC_QUESTION:NEXT I
       670   GOTO 850
       680   DEFPROC_BLOCK(X,Y,W,H)
       690   MOVE X,Y:MOVE X+W,Y
       700   PLOT 85,X,Y+H
       710   PLOT 85,X+W,Y+H
       720   ENDPROC
       730   DEFPROC_QUESTION
       740   IF I=1 THEN PT$="Head"
       750   IF I=2 THEN PT$="Arm "
       760   IF I=3 THEN PT$="Leg "
       770   PRINTTAB(0,2);PT$;" =":COLOUR 1:P
RINT"1 ";:COLOUR 2:PRINT"2 ";:COLOUR 3:P
RINT"3"
       780   PRINT TAB(0,4);"       ":PRINT"
       ":VDU 11:VDU 11
       790   T=1
       800   INPUT AN$:IF AN$ <> "1" AND AN$ <
> "2" AND AN$ <> "3" THEN PRINT "No";:VD
U 11:GOTO 800
       810   IF VAL(AN$) = W(I) THEN PRINT"Yes
       ":GOTO 840
       820   PRINT"No,try again":IF T=1 THEN V
DU 11:VDU 11:T=2:GOTO 800
       830   IF T=2 THEN VDU 11:PRINT"Answer =
 ";W(I);"   ":A$=INKEY$(500):GOTO 840
       840   ENDPROC
       850   REM
```

PROFIT AND LOSS

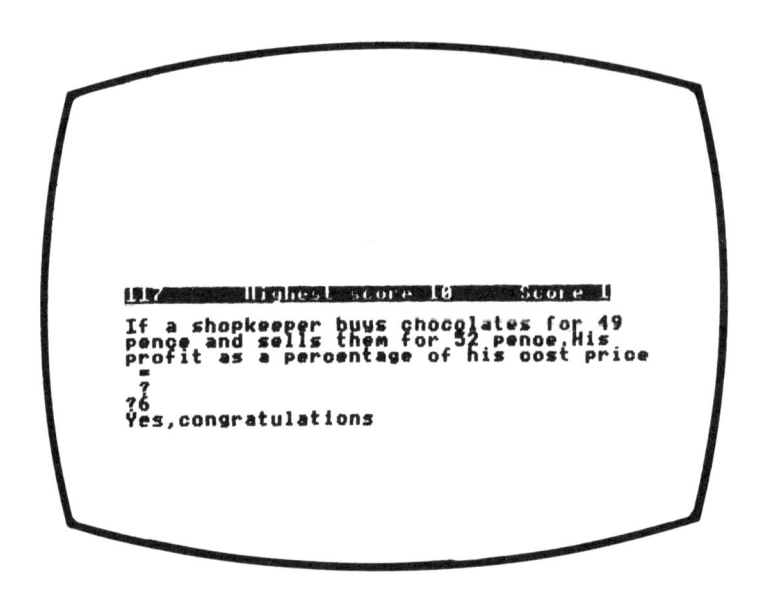

```
117        Highest score 10        Score 1
If a shopkeeper buys chocolates for 19
pence and sells them for 32 pence,his
profit as a percentage of his cost price
=
?
?6
Yes,congratulations
```

How much do you know about profit and loss?

Do you know how much you would make if you sold your car, or even your bike?

How to play

You will be given five minutes to answer as many questions as possible, and you may press P and RETURN for pass if you cannot work out an answer.

You will not be penalised for 'passes'.

At the end of five minutes, or sooner if you enter N for NO in answer to the question "do you want any more", your score sheet showing tries, correct answers and average time per answer will appear. If you wish to proceed, then press Y and RETURN and the program will continue to ask you questions.

You can have two tries at each question if you wish. After the first attempt, you will be given a hint as to the correct answer. If your second answer is wrong, you will be told the solution and how it was obtained.

If you cannot work out an answer then press ? and RETURN and your computer will turn into a calculator and you can then use the normal mathematical symbols on the keyboard. To clear the calculator from the screen press AC and RETURN. For the calculators answer press = and RETURN. To return to the main game press ? and RETURN. Always remember to press RETURN after each required response.

Programming hints

This program includes a useful procedure that enables a programmer to fit a sentence, or string, of any length onto a screen of any size, without splitting a word between one screen line and another, i.e. wraparound. This procedure is called PROC_FITIN and is found on line 530.

Assign the string, or sentence in quotes, to variable FL$. B holds the number of characters on the screen in the case of Mode 4 it is 40. On exit the field FL$ contains the string, or sentence, re-formatting so no words are split between one 40 column line and another.

You may want to add some different types of problems on profit and loss. To do this, instead of W alternating between -1 and +1, it should be allowed to take a random value between 0 and one more than the number of problem types you are going to add. The details of the problem must be put in the PROC_QUESTION procedure. Q$ holds the question, H$ the hint, A and A$ the answer and L$, M$ and N$ the answer and explanation.

```
10      REM QUIZ            - PROFIT AND LO
SS
20      REM COPYRIGHT (C) G.LUDINSKI 1983
30        MODE 4
40      DIM IP$(255)
50      S$=" "
60      HC$=" Highest score ":HK$="    S
core "
70        COLOUR 1:COLOUR 129:PRINT:PRIN
T:PRINT:PRINT"       Quiz game 1 - Profit
 and Loss"
80 PRINT:PRINT
90      INPUT"Hello,what is your name ",N
AM$:PRINT:PRINT"Here are some Problems "
;:IF NAM$<>"NO SOUND" THEN PRINTNAM$ ELS
E PRINT
100       TIME=0:P=0:MAX=0:C=0:W=1
110     T=1:I$=""
120     P=P+1
130     PROC_QUESTION
140     PRINT:PRINT
150         PRINT:PRINTQ$;" = ";
160     PROC_KEYIN:PRINT
170       IF I$="?" THEN PROC_CALC
180     IF ABS(VAL(I$)-A)<= X AND I$<>""
THEN GOTO 200
190     GOTO 220
200       PRINT: PRINT"Yes,congratulations
":C=C+1:PRINT:IF NAM$="NO SOUND" THEN GO
TO 250
210       SOUND1,-10,12,10:SOUND1,-10,20,1
0:SOUND1,-10,28,10:SOUND1,-10,32,20:SOUN
D1,-10,14,20:GOTO 250
220     IF T=1 THEN PRINT:PRINT"No,"H$",t
ry again":T=2:RB$=INKEY$(3000):CLS:PRINT
:PRINT:GOTO 150
230     PRINT:PRINT"Sorry,the answer is =
":PRINT:PRINT L$:PRINT:PRINT M$
240     PRINT:PRINTN$
250     IF TIME >= 30000 THEN PROC_SCORE
260     PRINT:PRINT"Do you want more ? (Y
/N)":PROC_KEYIN:PRINT
270     IF I$<>"Y" AND I$<>"N" AND I$<>""
 AND I$<>"YES" AND I$<>"NO" THEN GOTO 26
0
280     IF I$="Y" OR I$="YES" OR I$="" T
HEN T=1:CLS:GOTO 110
290     PROC_SCORE
300     GOTO 900
310     REM
320     DEFPROC_QUESTION
330       L$="":M$="":N$="":B=40:X=1
340     E=RND(9):F=INT(RND(1)*90+10):E$=S
TR$(E):F$=STR$(F)
```

```
350     W=-W
360     IF W=1 THEN GOTO 430
370     FL$="If a shopkeeper buys chocola
tes for "+F$+" pence and sells them for
"+STR$(E+F)+" pence.His Profit as a perc
entage of his cost price"
380     PROC_FITIN:Q$=FL$
390     H$="Percentage Profit =
            ((sell - cost) / cost) x 100 %
            where sell = selling Price
            and    cost = cost Price"
400     A=INT(E/F*100):A$=STR$(A)
410     L$=A$+" %"
420     M$="as ((("+STR$(E+F)+" - "+F$+")/
"+F$+") x 100 % = "+STR$(INT(E/F*100))
430     IF W=-1 THEN GOTO 520
440     V=E*100:V$=STR$(V)
450     FL$="A dealer wishes to make a Pr
ofit of "+F$+"%.If the car cost him \"+V
$+" then his selling price must be"
460     PROC_FITIN:Q$=FL$
470     H$="find the profit in money term
s.Then  add it to the cost price"
480     A=INT(V+(F*E)):A$=STR$(A):R1$=STR
$(INT(F*E))
490     L$="\"+A$
500     M$="as Profit = ("+F$+"/100) x "+
V$+"  = \"+R1$
510     N$="so selling Price = "+V$+" + "
+R1$+" = \"+A$
520     ENDPROC
530     DEFPROC_FITIN
540        LF=LEN(FL$):IF LF<= B THEN GOTO
620
550     FOR I=1 TO INT(LF/40)
560        EL=B*I
570           IF MID$(FL$,EL,1)=" "THEN GOTO
610
580           IF MID$(FL$,EL+1,1)=" " THEN FL
$=LEFT$(FL$,EL)+RIGHT$(FL$,LF-EL-1):LF=L
F-1:GOTO 610
590           FOR K=1 TO 39:IF MID$(FL$,EL-K,
1)=" " THEN FL$=LEFT$(FL$,EL-K)+LEFT$(S$
,K)+RIGHT$(FL$,LF-EL+K):LF=LF+K:GOTO 610
600              NEXT K
610        NEXT I
620     ENDPROC
630     END
640     DEFPROC_CALC
650        VP=VPOS:PRINT TAB(0,22);"
    Calculator mode              ";TAB(0,
22)
660     B$=""
670     I$=GET$:PRINTI$;:B$=B$+I$:IFI$ <>
"="ANDI$ <> "?"ANDB$<>"AC"THENGOTO670
680     IF B$="?"ORI$="?"THENGOTO720
690     IFB$="AC"THENPRINTTAB(0,23);S$;TA
B(0,22):B$="":GOTO660
700     IFLEN(B$)<=1THENGOTO660
710     PRINTEVAL LEFT$(B$,LEN(B$)-1);TAB
(0,22):GOTO660
720        PRINTTAB(0,22);S$;S$;TAB(0,VP-
1):PROC_KEYIN:PRINT
730     ENDPROC
740     DEFPROC_KEYIN
750     IX=1:VP=VPOS:HP=POS
760        IP$(IX)=INKEY$(10):IF IP$(IX)="
" THEN COLOUR 0:COLOUR 129:PRINT TAB(0,1
);INT(TIME/100);"         ";HC$;MAX;HK$;C:CO
```

```
LOUR 1:COLOUR 128:GOTO 760
   770      PRINT TAB(IX+HP,VP);IP$(IX); :IX
=IX+1:IP$(IX)=GET$:IF IP$(IX) <> CHR$(13
) THEN GOTO 770
   780    I$="":FOR I=1 TO IX-1:I$=I$+IP$(
I):NEXTI
   790    ENDPROC
   800    DEFPROC_SCORE
   810    CLS
   820    PRINT:PRINT
   830    PRINT:PRINT"Number of Problems co
mpleted = ";P
   840    PRINT:PRINT"Number correct = ";C
   850    TM=INT(TIME/100):PRINT:PRINT"Time
 taken in seconds = ";TM
   860    IF C <> 0 THEN PRINT:PRINT"Time
per problem = ";INT(TM/C)
   870    IF C > MAX THEN MAX=C
   880    TIME=0:P=0:C=0
   890    ENDPROC
   900    REM
```

ODD ONE OUT

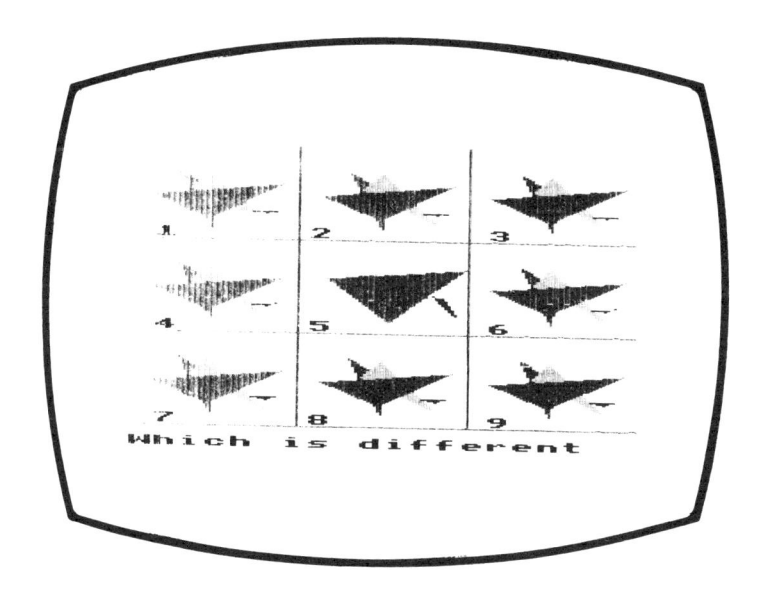

Nine patterns are displayed on the screen and you are given only a few seconds to compare them and identify the odd one out.

A score sheet will be displayed, showing the number of puzzles completed, number correct and the time and average time taken.

How to play

Each of the patterns on the screen will be identified by a number, and you must key in the appropriate number as your guess.

If you get the answer wrong, you will be told the correct

answer, to the accompaniment of a rather low pitched little tune. Get it right, however, and you will hear a pleasant little tune.

After each attempt you will be asked if you wish more (Y for Yes) or wish to stop (N for No).

Remember to press RETURN.

Programming hints

The filled in triangles are drawn by MOVEing to one point, them MOVEing to another point, then drawing a line to a third point using PLOT 85, and this fills in the space between the first point and the line between the second and third points. This is done in the procedure PROC_PATTERN. The pattern is transferred across and down the screen by adding the appropriate XD or YD or both, depending on the position of the screen.

You could put some more triangles into each pattern by increasing the maximum value of L in procedure PROC PATTERN. You would also have to reDIMension arrays X,Y and C in line 30. Also the maximum value of I should be increased in line 230.

```
 10    REM ODD ONE OUT
 20    REM COPYRIGHT (C) G.LUDINSKI 1983
 30    DIM X(4,3),Y(4,3),C(4)
 40    MODE 5
 50    NU=0:CR=0
 60    TIME=0
 70    CLS
 80    NU=NU+1
 90    PT=0
100    REM
110    REM DRAW FRAMEWORK
120    REM
130    GCOL 0,2:COLOUR 3
140    MOVE 426,255:DRAW 426,1023
150    MOVE 852,255:DRAW 852,1023
160    MOVE 0,255:DRAW 1279,255
170    MOVE 0,510:DRAW 1279,510
180    MOVE 0,765:DRAW 1279,765
190    REM
200    REM GENERATE SHAPES
210    REM
220    W=INT(RND(1)*6+1)
```

```
230    FOR I=1 TO 4
240      C(I)=INT(RND(1)*3+1)
250      FOR J=1 TO 3
260        X(I,J)=INT(RND(1)*370+30)
270        Y(I,J)=INT(RND(1)*200+30)
280      NEXT J
290    NEXT I
300  REM
310  REM DRAW PATTERNS
320  REM
330  FOR J=765 TO 255 STEP -255
340    FOR I=0 TO 852 STEP 426
350      PROC_PATTERN(I,J)
360    NEXT I
370  NEXT J
380  REM
390  REM QUESTION
400  REM
410  PRINT TAB(0,25);"Which is different ";
420  I$="":I=0
430  I$=INKEY$(0):IF I$ = "" AND I < 300 THEN I=I+1:GOTO 430
440  IF I$ <> "" AND (I$ < STR$(1) OR I$ > STR$(9)) THEN GOTO 430
450  IF VAL(I$)=W THEN PRINT:PRINT"Yes, you are right":SOUND 1,-15,101,30:CR=CR+1:GOTO 470
460  PRINT:PRINT"No, ";W;" is different":SOUND 1,-15,73,10:SOUND 1,-15,69,5
470  PRINT:PRINT"Do you want more Y/N";
480  INPUT R$
490  IF R$ <> "N" THEN GOTO 70
500  REM
510  REM SCORE SHEET
520  REM
530  CLS
540  PRINT:PRINT"     Odd one out"
550  FOR I=1 TO 9:PRINT:NEXT I
560  PRINT:PRINT"Problems completed =";NU
570  TM=INT(TIME/100)
580  PRINT:PRINT"Problems correct = ";CR
590  PRINT:PRINT"Time taken = ";TM:PRINT"secs"
600  IF CR <> 0 THEN PRINT:PRINT"Time / Problem = ";INT(TM/CR):PRINT"secs"
610  GOTO 750
620  REM
630  DEFPROC_PATTERN(XD,YD)
640  PT=PT+1
650  PRINT TAB((20*XD/1279)+1,31-(32*YD)/1023);PT
660  H1=0:H2=0:H3=0
670  IF PT=W THEN H1=INT(RND(1)*25+10):H2=INT(RND(1)*25+10):H3=INT(RND(1)*25+10)
680  FOR L=1 TO 4
690    GCOL 0,C(L)
700    MOVE (X(L,1)+XD+H1),(Y(L,1)+YD+H1)
710    MOVE (X(L,2)+XD+H2),(Y(L,2)+YD+H1)
720    PLOT 85,(X(L,3)+XD+H3),(Y(L,3)+YD-H1)
730  NEXT L
740  ENDPROC
750  REM END
```

DECISIVE HERO

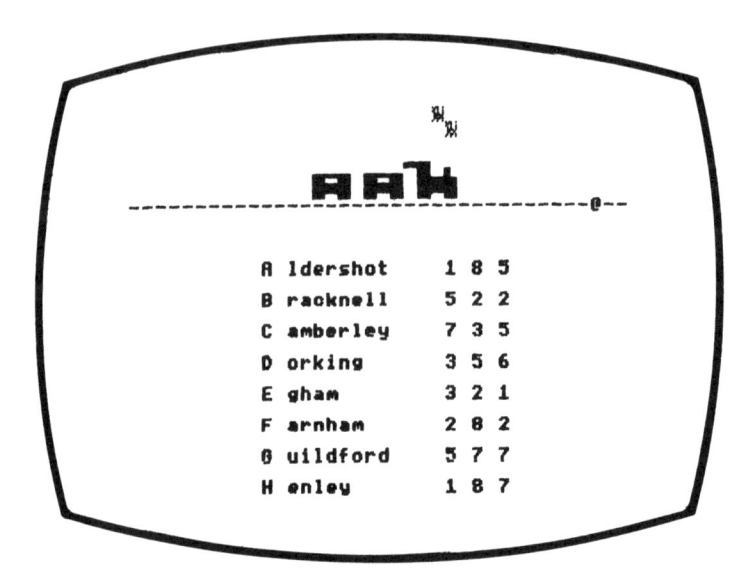

```
              ж
              ж
        ┌─┐┌─┐┐ ┐
────────┤ ││ │┤ ├──────────────── e ──
        └─┘└─┘┴ ┴

        A ldershot    1 8 5
        B racknell    5 2 2
        C amberley    7 3 5
        D orking      3 5 6
        E gham        3 2 1
        F arnham      2 8 2
        G uildford    5 7 7
        H enley       1 8 7
```

The wicked Baron has captured your love, Loretta, and tied her to the railroad track. Only you can save her from a grisly fate, but you will have to think fast and act even quicker. Wherever the Baron has taken her, you can be sure that it will be in a town far away from you, and you must work out the three possibilities, key in your answers and stop the train.

Please act quickly, as the thought of losing Loretta is too terrible to contemplate.

How to play

The names of eight towns will be displayed on the screen with letters A to H. Against each of the letters you will be shown a combination of numbers.

You must decide which three series of numbers are the highest, type them in and stop the train.

Example: from the screen shown above you will see that the correct answer is C, G and H. You don't have to key in your answers in alphabetical order, just key them in correctly and quickly. If you stop the train or, unfortunately for Loretta, the train reaches the end of the screen, you will be asked if you wish to continue or end the program.

Press C and RETURN to continue, or E and RETURN to end the game.

Skill rating

When the game ends, a score sheet will be displayed showing your total, giving a qualitative rating and an IQ level of your decisiveness. This is not a true IQ level as intelligence is made up of reasoning ability, memory etc. but this result will be an indication of your IQ decisiveness level.

Classifications below Fair are omitted, as I know that if you are using this book you are above average!

Programming hints

The number of carriages pulled by the engine can be increased by adding more sets of a space and CA$ to line 250.

CA$ is a shape for the carriage top.

You must also add the same number of sets of a space and CR$ in line 260.

CR$ is the shape for the carriage bottom.

Count the number of characters you have added and add the same number of spaces to A$(1) in line 240.

Remember also to alter the TR$ in line 960 as this effects the backspace characters required.

Before you decide to increase the number of carriages, remember that the more carriages there are, the closer the head of the train is to Loretta.

After thinking about this, you may decide to **reduce** the number of carriages and thereby increase your thinking time.

```
 10    REM DECISIVE HERO
 20    REM COPYRIGHT (C) G.LUDINSKI 1983
 30    MODE 4
 40    DIM A$(3),X(12),Y(12),N(3,8),S(8)
,T$(8),TW(8)
 50    CLS
 60    S$="     "
 70    REM
 80    REM CURSOR MOVEMENT AND SHAPE DEF
INITIONS
 90    REM
 100    VDU 23,224,255,255,255,255,255,25
5,255,255
 110    VDU 23,225,0,0,0,255,255,255,255,
255
 120    VDU 23,226,0,0,0,255,255,0,0,0
 130    VDU 23,227,255,255,255,255,255,0,
0,0
 140    VDU 23,228,0,0,0,0,0,255,255,255
 150    VDU 23,229,240,240,240,240,240,25
5,255,255
 160    VDU 19,0,4,0,0,0
 170    CB$=CHR$(8):CU$=CHR$(11)
 180    G0$=CHR$(224):G1$=CHR$(225):G2$=C
HR$(226):G3$=CHR$(227):CA$=G1$+G2$+G1$:C
R$=G0$+G3$+G0$
 190    D$="  "+CHR$(175)
 200    REM
 210    REM STORE TOWN NAMES AND TRAIN SH
APE
 220    REM
 230    RESTORE:FOR I=1 TO 8:READ T$(I):N
EXT I
 240    A$(1)=LEFT$(S$,8)+CHR$(228)+CHR$(
228)+"    "
 250    A$(2)="    "+CA$+"  "+CA$+"  "+G0$+CHR
$(228)+CHR$(229)
 260    A$(3)="    "+CR$+"  "+CR$+"  "+CR$
 270    REM
 280    REM STORE POSITIONS OF SMOKE
 290    REM
 300    FOR I=1 TO 2
```

```
310     X(I)=12-I
320     Y(I)=2-I
330     NEXT I
340   FOR I=3 TO 12
350     Y(I)=2
360     X(I)=13-I
370     NEXT I
380   TE=0:ER=0:CR=0
390   REM
400   REM THE ACTION STARTS HERE
410   REM
420   CLS
430   TE=TE+1
440   REM
450   REM STORE LISTS OF NUMBERS AND TH
EIR SUMS
460   REM
470   FOR K=1 TO 7:S(K)=0:NEXT K
480   FOR J=1 TO 8
490     FOR I=1 TO 3
500       N(I,J)=INT(RND(1)*9+1)
510       S(J)=S(J)+N(I,J)
520     NEXT I
530   NEXT J
540   FOR I=1 TO 8:TW(I)=I:NEXT I
550   REM
560   REM  BUBBLE SORT OF THE SUMS OF E
ACH LIST
570   REM
580   FOR J=1 TO 6
590     FOR I=1 TO 7
600       IF S(I) < S(I+1) THEN TP=S(I)
:S(I)=S(I+1):S(I+1)=TP:TP=TW(I):TW(I)=TW
(I+1):TW(I+1)=TP
610     NEXT I
620   NEXT J
630   REM
640   REM CHECK FOR ANY DUPLICATES
650   REM
660   TWN=3:FOR I=4 TO 8
670     IF S(I)=S(1) OR S(I)=S(2) OR S(
I)=S(3) THEN TWN=I
680   NEXT I
690   REM
700   REM DISPLAY PROBLEM
710   REM
720   PRINT:PRINT:PRINT:PRINT:PRINT:PRI
NT
730   PRINT "---------------------------
---------","@","--"
740   PRINT:PRINT:PRINT
750   FOR J=1 TO 8
760     PRINT LEFT$(S$,10);LEFT$(T$(J),
1);" ";RIGHT$(T$(J),9);"    ";
770     FOR I=1 TO 3
780       PRINT STR$(N(I,J));" ";
790     NEXT I
800     PRINT:PRINT
810   NEXT J
820   PRINT
830   CR1=0
840   VDU 30:PROCTRAIN
850   SOUND1,-10,32,10:SOUND1,-10,14,10
860   *FX 15,1
870   PRINT TAB(0,28);"Press C to conti
nue or E to end program":INPUT C$
880   IF C$="C" THEN GOTO 420
890   PROCIQ
900   GOTO 1400
```

```
910    REM
920    DEFPROCSMOKE
930    PRINTTAB(X(I)+L,Y(I));G$
940    ENDPROC
950    DEFPROCTRAIN
960    TR$=A$(1)+CHR$(10)+STRING$(12,CHR
$(8))+A$(2)+CHR$(10)+STRING$(12,CHR$(8))
+A$(3)
970    FOR L=1 TO 24
980      I$=INKEY$(0)
990      IF I$="" THEN GOTO 1040
1000     FOR J=1 TO TWN
1010       IF I$=CHR$(64+TW(J)) THEN CR1
=CR1+1:SOUND 1,-15,81,10:GOTO 1040
1020     NEXT J
1030     ER=ER+1
1040     IF CR1=3 THEN CR=CR+1:GOTO 1240
1050     PRINT TAB(L,3);" "TR$;
1060     SOUND 0,-15,100,2
1070     I=1
1080     G$=D$
1090     PROCSMOKE
1100     I=I+1
1110     G$=D$
1120     PROCSMOKE
1130     G$="  "
1140     I=I-1
1150     PROCSMOKE
1160     I=I+1
1170     G$=D$
1180     IF I < 12 THEN GOTO 1100
1190     G$="  "
1200     I=9
1210     PROCSMOKE
1220     G$=" "+CHR$(175)
1230    NEXT L
1240    ENDPROC
1250    DEFPROCIQ
1260    CLS
1270    PRINT:PRINT"Number of tests compl
eted = ";TE
1280    PRINT:PRINT"Number of tests corre
ct = ";CR
1290    PRINT:PRINT"Number of incorrect a
nswers = ";ER
1300    SC=INT(((ER*3)+((TE-CR)*10))/TE)
1310    PRINT
1320    IF SC < 5 THEN PRINT"This is cla
ssed as SUPERIOR (upper 10%)":GOTO 1350
1330    IF SC < 7 THEN PRINT"This is cla
ssed as GOOD (upper 30%)":GOTO 1350
1340    IF SC < 9 THEN PRINT"This is cla
ssed as FAIR (upper 60%)"
1350    IF SC=0 THEN IQU=150:GOTO 1370
1360    IQU=INT(760/SC):IF IQU > 150 THEN
 IQU=150
1370    PRINT:PRINT"Your I.Q. level (deci
siveness) = ";IQU
1380    ENDPROC
1390    DATA "Aldershot ","Bracknell ","C
amberley ","Dorking   ","Egham     ","Fa
rnham    ","Guildford ","Henley    "
1400    REM END
```

FRACTION CAR CHASE

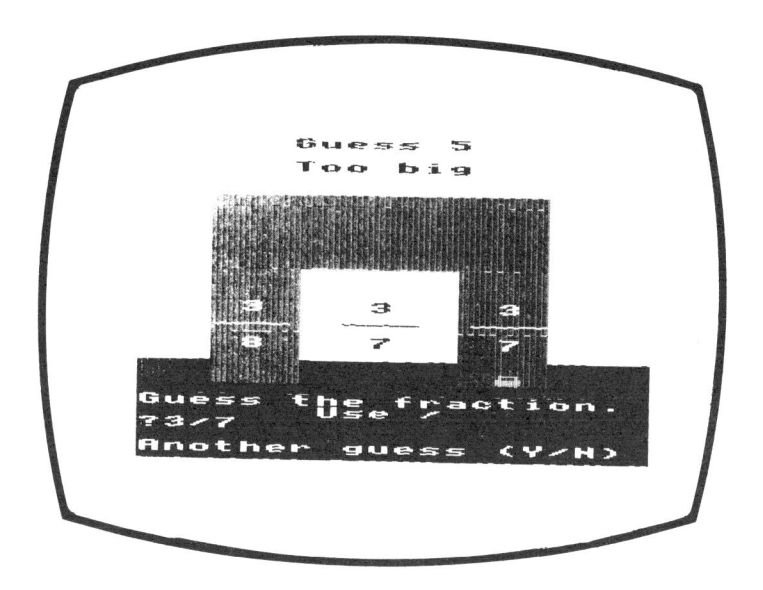

We might have named this program 'Duel' after the film of the same name as, like the hero of the film, you are being chased by a juggernaut driver.

As you turn right, the juggernaut turns right; turn left and it still follows you.

Coming up in the near distance is an archway. You **must** escape through the arch before the lumbering truck rolls over you.

Your only answer is to work out how far across the road the centre of the arch is. Guess wrongly and you hit the arch damaging your car. Too many wrong guesses and your car will be immobilised leaving you the defenceless victim of the fast approaching juggernaut.

How to play

The computer will think of a number whose numerator (top half) and denominator (bottom half) are both ten or less. You must guess the correct fraction and enter it in using the / symbol (eg 2/3) and RETURN. If your guess is too big, or small, you will be told. The guess closest to the correct answer, will be displayed on the arch. The lower guess will be shown on the left hand pillar and the higher guess, closest to the correct answer, will be shown on the right hand pillar.

If your answer is displayed on the arch then you know that you are almost correct. You have nine lives.

This is more difficult than it sounds, after all do you know which is the larger, 3/8 or 4/9? You will be amazed at what you find out about fractions. A hint is that to make a fraction bigger, increase its numerator (top half) or reduce its denominator (bottom half) or both. Do the opposite to make a fraction smaller.

Programming hints

To make the game easier, reduce the range of fractions allowed. This is done by reducing the tens in line 230. To make it more difficult you may increase these numbers to maximum values of 99 each.

If you want to allow more guesses, increase the 9 in line 280.

```
10  REM FRACTION CAR CHASE
20  REM COPYRIGHT (C) G.LUDINSKI 1983
30  MODE 5
40  VDU 19,0,4,0,0,0
50  CLS
60  GOTO 130
70  DEF FNB(N$)
80  TF=0
90  FOR L=0 TO 7
```

```
100     TF=TF+(2^L)*VAL(MID$(N$,8-L,1))
110     NEXT L
120    =TF
130     VDU 23,224,FNB("01111110"),FNB("0
1000010"),FNB("01000010"),255,255,255,25
5,FNB("01000010")
140     COLOUR 128:CLS:MAX=1:MIN=0:CA$=CH
R$(224):M1$="0":M2$=" ":X1$="1":X2$=" "
150     REM
160     REM DRAW ARCH
170     REM
180     GCOL 0,3:PROC_BLOCK(0,0,1280,350)
190     GCOL 0,2:PROC_BLOCK(190,290,210,5
10):PROC_BLOCK(800,290,220,510):PROC_BLO
CK(190,600,830,200)
200     REM
210     REM THINK OF FRACTION
220     REM
230     F=RND(10):G=RND(10)
240     PROC_REDUCE
250     IF F=G OR F/G=INT(F/G) OR G/F=INT
(G/F) THEN GOTO 230
260     IF G < F THEN H=G:G=F:F=H
270     COLOUR 131:COLOUR 1:PRINT TAB(9,
23);CA$
280     FOR T=1 TO 9
290       COLOUR 131:COLOUR 0:PRINT TAB(0
,24);STRING$(120," ");
300       PRINT TAB(0,24);"Guess the frac
tion.    Use /"
310       INPUT I$:IF I$="" THEN GOTO 310

320       REM
330       REM CHECK ENTRY
340       REM
350       FOR I=1 TO LEN(I$)
360         C$=MID$(I$,I,1)
370         IF (C$ < "0" OR C$ > "9") AND
C$ <> "/" THEN GOTO 400
380         IF C$="/" AND I > 1 AND LEN(I
$) > 2 THEN NM$=LEFT$(I$,I-1):DN$=RIGHT
$(I$,LEN(I$)-I):GOTO 410
390       NEXT I
400       VDU 11:SOUND 1,-15,50,10:GOTO 3
10
410       IF LEN(NM$) > 2 OR LEN(DN$) > 2
THEN GOTO 400
420       REM
430       REM DISPLAY FRACTION BETWEEN AR
CH
440       REM
450       COLOUR 128:COLOUR 3:PRINT TAB(9
,16);"  ":PRINT TAB(9,16);NM$:PRINT TAB(
8,17);"___":PRINT TAB(9,19);"  ":PRINT T
AB(9,19);DN$
460       COLOUR 128:COLOUR 3:PRINT TAB(6
,2);"Guess ";T
470       IF NM$=STR$(F) AND DN$=STR$(G)
THEN PRINT:PRINT"     That's right":PROC_
CAR(" ",CA$," "):GOTO 600
480       IF NM$="0" OR DN$="0" THEN GOTO
 400
490       VI=EVAL(I$)
500       COLOUR 131:PRINT TAB(9,23);" ":
COLOUR 128
510       IF VI < F/G THEN PRINT TAB(6,4)
```

```
          ;"Too small":PROC_CAR(CA$," "," ")
   520       IF VI > F/G THEN PRINT TAB(6,4)
;"Too big   ":PROC_CAR(" "," ",CA$)
   530       IF VI < MAX AND VI > F/G THEN M
AX=VI:X1$=NM$:X2$=DN$
   540       IF VI > MIN AND VI < F/G THEN M
IN=VI:M1$=NM$:M2$=DN$
   550       COLOUR 0:COLOUR 130:PRINT TAB(4
,16);"    ":PRINT TAB(4,16);M1$
   560       IF M2$ <> " " THEN PRINT TAB(3,
17);"___":PRINT TAB(4,19);"    ":PRINT TAB
(4,19);M2$
   570       PRINT TAB(14,16);"    ":PRINT TAB
(14,16);X1$
   580       IF X2$ <> " " THEN PRINT TAB(13
,17);"___":PRINT TAB(14,19);"    ":PRINT T
AB(14,19);X2$
   590       GOTO 610
   600       COLOUR 0:COLOUR 131:PRINT TAB(0
,24);STRING$(120," "):PRINT TAB(0,24);"Y
ou escaped - phew!":GOTO 700
   610       COLOUR 131:PRINT TAB(0,28);"Ano
ther guess (Y/N) ";
   620       INPUT R$
   630       IF R$="N" THEN GOTO 680
   640       NEXT T
   650    REM
   660    REM END OF GUESSES
   670    REM
   680       COLOUR 0:COLOUR 131:PRINT TAB(0,2
4);STRING$(120," "):PRINT TAB(0,24);"The
 juggernaut       closes in"
   690    PRINT:PRINT"The fraction is        "
;F;"/";G
   700    PRINT:PRINT"Do you want more Y/N"
;
   710    INPUT R$:IF R$ <> "N" THEN GOTO 1
40
   720    GOTO 870
   730    STOP
   740    DEFPROC_BLOCK(X,Y,W,H)
   750    MOVE X,Y:MOVE X+W,Y
   760    PLOT 85,X,Y+H
   770    PLOT 85,X+W,Y+H
   780    ENDPROC
   790    DEFPROC_CAR(P1$,P2$,P3$)
   800    COLOUR 130:COLOUR 1:PRINT TAB(4,2
2);P1$;:COLOUR 131:PRINT TAB(9,22);P2$;:
COLOUR 130:PRINT TAB(14,22);P3$;
   810    ENDPROC
   820    DEFPROC_REDUCE
   830    FOR I=2 TO 9
   840       IF F/I = INT(F/I) AND G/I = INT
(G/I) THEN F=F/I:G=G/I:GOTO 840
   850       NEXT I
   860    ENDPROC
   870    END
```

WESTERN ADVENTURE GAME

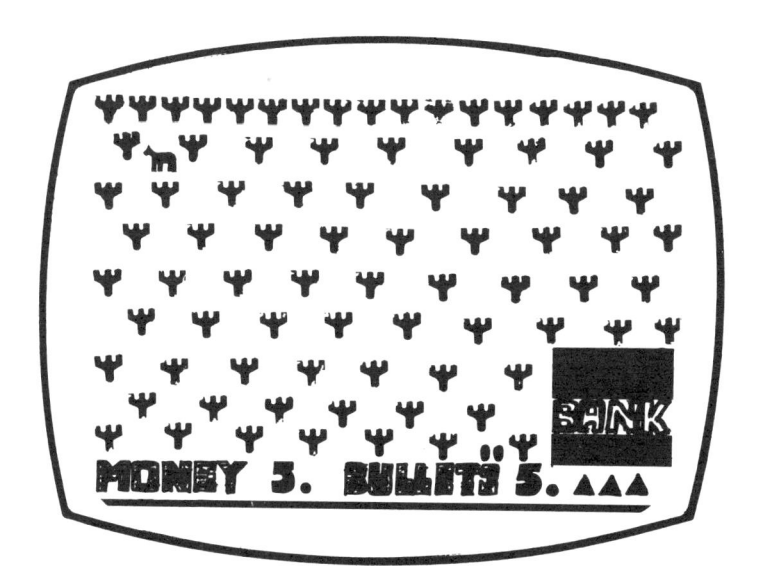

Your rough, tough and ready desperado colleagues have fled into the scrubland, dropping their guns and the loot.

Well we all know that a man, or a Calamity Jane, has got to do what ever it is. So, you are on your own outside the bank and you have to make it to the horses, which some idiot left on the outskirts of town.

On the way you can collect money and guns with bullets and then decide, if you run into the Sheriff's posse, whether to bribe or blast your way to freedom. Obviously your aim is to reach the horses with some bullets and some money.

We are not advocating here that crime pays — that is up to you.

How to play

Use the ARROW keys to make your moves.

Your footsteps will appear on the screen as you move toward the horse in the top left hand corner of the screen.

Your progress will be recorded on the bottom of the screen, and you will, in your progress, be told that you have run into the posse, and you will then be asked if you intend to shoot or bribe your way out.

Key in SHOOT or BRIBE

Should you run out of bullets I'm afraid that a lynching is your fate, as the posse were playing poker when you robbed the bank, and the Sheriff had a Royal Flush.

To exit from the game press the BREAK key.

Programming hints

You can increase the number of events in the adventure by allowing W on line 450, to be larger.

A procedure describing the event, and the effect of it, on the money and bullets can be written.

The new procedures can be listed after line 490.

Remember that

> BU is number of bullets

MO is money
X is the random amount to increase/decrease

```
10    REM WESTERN ADVENTURE GAME
20    REM COPYRIGHT (C) G.LUDINSKI 1983
30    *KEY 10 "OLDIM"
40    MODE 5
50    X0=13:Y0=22
60    VDU 19,3,2,0,0,0
70    COLOUR 128:COLOUR 2
80    CLS
90    GCOL 0,1
100   REM
110   REM BINARY TO DECIMAL CONVERSION
FOR USER DEFINED GRAPHICS
120   REM
130   DEF FNH(N$)=VAL(RIGHT$(N$,1))+2*V
AL(MID$(N$,7,1))+4*VAL(MID$(N$,6,1))+8*V
AL(MID$(N$,5,1))+16*VAL(MID$(N$,4,1))+32
*VAL(MID$(N$,3,1))+64*VAL(MID$(N$,2,1))+
128*VAL(LEFT$(N$,1))
140   REM
150   REM CACTUS
160   REM
170   VDU 23,225,FNH("11011011"),FNH("1
1011011"),FNH("11011011"),255,255,FNH("0
0011000"),FNH("00011000"),FNH("00011000"
)
180   COLOUR 3:FOR I=1 TO 150:PRINTCHR$
(225);" ";:NEXT I:COLOUR 2
190   REM
200   REM DRAW BANK
210   REM
220   PROC_BLOCK(940,280,279,300)
230   COLOUR 129:PRINTTAB(15,18);"BANK"
:COLOUR 128
240   REM
250   REM HORSE
260   REM
270   VDU 23,224,0,0,FNH("01100000"),FN
H("01110000"),FNH("01011111"),FNH("00011
111"),FNH("00010001"),FNH("00010001")
280   COLOUR 1:PRINTTAB(1,2);CHR$(224):
COLOUR 2
290   REM
300   REM WRITE MESSAGES
310   REM
320   BU=5:MO=5:DI=1
330   PROC_BLANK:PRINTTAB(0,24);DI;" > "
;" Money    Bullets":PRINTTAB(6,25);MO;"
      ";BU
340   IF BU <= 0 THEN PRINT:PRINT"You g
et shot.You    have travelled ";DI;" yds
":GOTO 780
350   X=INT(RND(1)*5+2)
360   *FX4,1
370   TU$=GET$
380   IF TU$ < CHR$(136) OR TU$ > CHR$(
139) THEN GOTO 370
390   IF TU$ = CHR$(136) THEN X0=X0-1
400   IF TU$ = CHR$(137) THEN X0=X0+1
410   IF TU$ = CHR$(138) THEN Y0=Y0+1
420   IF TU$ = CHR$(139) THEN Y0=Y0-1
430   PRINTTAB(X0,Y0);"*";
```

```
440   DI=DI+1
450   W=INT(RND(1)*4+1)
460   COLOUR 1
470   IF W=1 THEN PROC_POSSE
480   IF W=2 THEN PROC_BULLETS
490   IF W=3 THEN PROC_MONEY
500   COLOUR 2
510   GOTO 330
520   REM
530   DEFPROC_POSSE:PRINT TAB(0,26)"You meet one of the sheriff's posse. Do you shoot or bribe ?"
540   INPUT I$
550   IF I$ <> "SHOOT" AND I$ <>"shoot" AND I$ <> "BRIBE" AND I$ <> "bribe" THEN VDU 11:GOTO 540
560   IF I$ = "SHOOT" OR I$ = "shoot" THEN BU=BU-X
570   IF I$ = "BRIBE" OR I$ = "bribe" THEN MO=MO-X
580   IF BU < 0 THEN BU=0
590   IF MO < 0 THEN MO=0
600   ENDPROC
610   DEFPROC_BULLETS:PRINT TAB(0,26);"You find ";X;" bullets that your gang left behind"
620   BU=BU+X
630   I$=GET$
640   ENDPROC
650   DEFPROC_MONEY:PRINT TAB(0,26);"You find ";X;" bags of money that your gang left behind"
660   MO=MO+X
670   I$=GET$
680   ENDPROC
690   DEFPROC_BLOCK(X,Y,W,H)
700   MOVE X,Y:MOVE X+W,Y
710   PLOT 85,X,Y+H
720   PLOT 85,X+W,Y+H
730   ENDPROC
740   DEFPROC_BLANK
750   S$="":FOR I = 1 TO 140:S$=S$+" ":NEXT I
760   PRINTTAB(1,24);S$;
770   ENDPROC
780   REM END
```

DETECTIVE

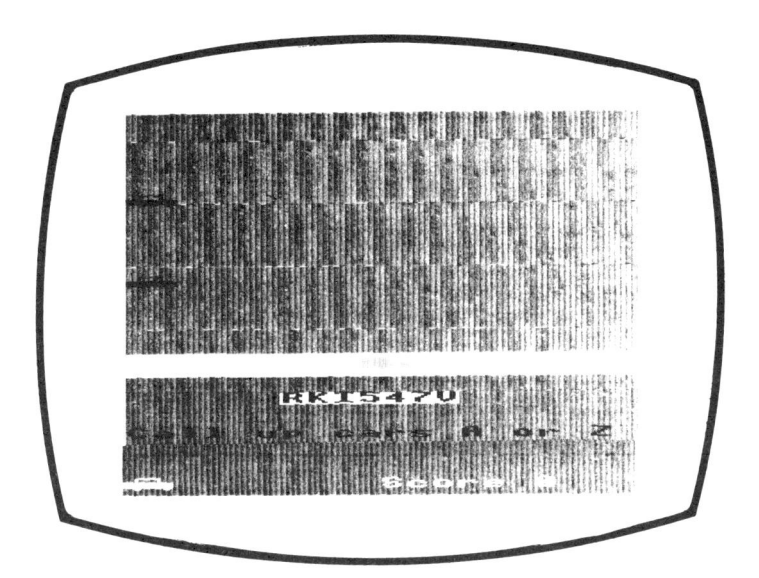

Could you solve the cases and survive the perils of being a detective. Find out by playing this game.

Firstly, you are briefed on the correct number-plates for the cars and trucks you are likely to see. Then you are stationed near a main road, watching cars and lorries travel past.

You are looking for a stolen vehicle whose plates have been changed. When you see a car or lorry you suspect, you must call up, by radio, the two squad cars in the area, and tell them to set up a road-block.

If you time it right, the suspected vehicle, which veers off the road when it sees you are interested, will be caught. If your suspected vehicle was stolen and you catch it, the driver comes quietly and your score increases. If however, you catch a vehicle which has not been stolen, the driver dresses you down, and your score decreases. If you do not catch the suspected vehicle, then you are told whether your suspicions were correct but your score is unchanged.

How to play

Press C when you have read which cars and lorries have which number plates. Then you see cars and lorries travel by with the number plates they have attached to them displayed below the road. When you see a vehicle which you suspect has the wrong number plate, then press A to get the white car at the top of the screen to set up a road block, or Z to have the other white car set up a trap. You may do this continuously, by trying to set up the road block just as the suspected vehicle passes by.

If you catch the vehicle you will hear police-car sirens as the other squad cars approach. Then you are told the result. Press the RETURN key to play again.

Programming hints

The cars and lorries are made up of two user-defined characters next to each other. They are animated, or made to travel along the road, in line 450. They are animated by PRINTing them in successive positions along the road, preceded by a space to erase the back half of the previously-drawn vehicle.

You can make the game more difficult by making the vehicles whizz past faster. To do this reduce the value of K in line 400.

```
10    REM DETECTIVE
20    REM COPYRIGHT (C) G.LUDINSKI 1983
30    MODE 5
40    DIM V$(6),C(6),P$(5),VM$(6)
50    B=128:BL=0:RD=1:GR=2:WH=3:SC=0
60    VDU 19,GR,2,0,0,0
70    GOTO 200
80    REM
90    REM U.D.G. CALCULATOR
100   REM REM
110   DEF FNB(N$)
120   TF=0
130   FOR L=0 TO 7
140     TF=TF+(2^L)*VAL(MID$(N$,8-L,1))
150   NEXT L
160   =TF
170   REM
180   REM CAR AND LORRY SHAPES
190   REM
200   VDU 23,224,FNB("00001111"),FNB("00001000"),FNB("00001000"),255,255,255,255,FNB("00001100")
210   VDU 23,225,FNB("11110000"),FNB("00010000"),FNB("00010000"),255,255,255,255,FNB("00000110")
220   VDU 23,226,FNB("11000000"),FNB("11111000"),FNB("11001000"),FNB("11001111"),255,255,255,FNB("11001110")
230   VDU 23,227,255,255,255,255,255,255,255,FNB("01110001")
240   CA$=CHR$(224)+CHR$(225):LO$=CHR$(227)+CHR$(226)
250   C(1)=WH:P$(1)=" "+CA$:C(2)=RD:P$(2)=" "+CA$:C(3)=GR:P$(3)=" "+CA$
260   FOR I=1 TO 3:C(I+3)=C(I):P$(I+3)=" "+LO$:NEXT I
270   PROC_START
280   REM
290   REM DRAW FIELDS,ROAD,POLICE CARS
300   REM
310   COLOUR B+BL:COLOUR WH:CLS
320   GCOL 0,GR:PROC_BLOCK(0,0,1280,1024)
330   GCOL 0,BL:PROC_BLOCK(0,300,1280,60)
340   PROC_MIX
350   COLOUR B+GR:COLOUR WH:PRINT TAB(0,7);CA$;TAB(0,14);CA$:COLOUR BL:PRINT TAB(0,30);CA$;TAB(10,30);"Score ";SC
360   COLOUR WH:PRINT TAB(0,27);"Call up cars A or Z "
370   REM
380   REM LET CARS TRAVEL ALONG ROAD
390   REM
400   COLOUR B+BL:K=20
410   J=RND(6)
420   FOR I=0 TO 17
430     IF I=0 THEN COLOUR C(J):PRINT TAB(I,21);P$(J):COLOUR B+BL:COLOUR WH:PRINT TAB(6,24);VM$(J):FOR D=1 TO 5000:NEXT D
440     COLOUR C(J)
450     I$=INKEY$(0):IF I$="" THEN PRINT TAB(I,21);P$(J):GOTO 480
460     IF I$="H" THEN PROC_START:GOTO 310
470     GOTO 510
480     FOR D =1 TO K:NEXTD
490     NEXT:COLOUR BL:PRINT TAB(17,21);"   ";
```

```
500     COLOUR WH:GOTO 410
510     PROC_CHASE
520     REM
530     REM FINAL MESSAGE AND POLICE SIREN
540     REM
550     COLOUR BL
560     IF EN=1 AND (VN$=VM$(A) OR VN$=VM$(BB)) THEN SC=SC+1:PRINT TAB(0,27);"It's a fair cop,guv.":GOTO 600
570     IF EN=1 THEN PRINT TAB(0,27);"I'll sue you,you b**":SC=SC-1:GOTO 600
580     IF VN$=VM$(A) OR VN$=VM$(BB) THEN PRINT TAB(0,27);"Stolen car has gone ":GOTO 600
590     PRINT TAB(0,27);"Chasing wrong car "
600     *FX15,0
610     FOR I=1 TO 4:SOUND 1,-15,109,10:SOUND 1,-15,101,10:NEXT
620     PRINT TAB(0,30);"Press RETURN       ";:INPUT RB$ :GOTO 270
630     REM
640     DEFPROC_BLOCK(X,Y,W,H)
650     MOVE X,Y:MOVE X+W,Y
660     PLOT 85,X,Y+H
670     PLOT 85,X+W,Y+H
680     ENDPROC
690     DEFPROC_START
700     COLOUR B+BL:CLS
710     FOR I=1 TO 6
720       V$(I)=CHR$(64+RND(26))+CHR$(64+RND(26))+CHR$(64+RND(26))+STR$(RND(10)-1)+STR$(RND(10)-1)+STR$(RND(10)-1)+CHR$(64+RND(26))
730     NEXT
740     FOR I=1 TO 6 STEP 2
750       COLOUR C(I):PRINT TAB(3,10+(4*INT((I-1)/2)));P$(I);:COLOUR C(I+1):PRINT TAB(12,10+(4*INT((I-1)/2)));P$(I+1)
760       COLOUR C(I):PRINT:PRINT "   ";V$(I)," ";:COLOUR C(I+1):PRINT V$(I+1):PRINT
770     NEXT I
780     COLOUR WH:PRINT TAB(0,27);"Press C to continue"
790     RB$=INKEY$(6000)
800     ENDPROC
810     DEFPROC_MIX
820     A=RND(6):BB=RND(6):IF BB=A THEN GOTO 820
830     FOR I=1 TO 6
840       VM$(I)=V$(I)
850     NEXT
860     WK$=VM$(A):VM$(A)=VM$(BB):VM$(BB)=WK$
870     ENDPROC
880     DEFPROC_CHASE
890     COLOUR B+BL:PRINT TAB(0,21),"               ";
900     COLOUR B+GR
910     CL=C(J):VT$=RIGHT$(P$(J),2):VN$=VM$(J)
920     X=2:Y=19:GO=0:X1=X:Y1=Y:EN=0
930     COLOUR WH:PRINT TAB(0,7);CA$
940     PRINT TAB(0,14);CA$
950     I$=INKEY$(0)
960     IF I$="A" THEN PROC_ROAD(7)
970     IF I$="Z" THEN PROC_ROAD(14)
```

```
980   IF EN=1 THEN GOTO 1080
990   COLOUR CL:PRINT TAB(X,Y);VT$;
1000  PRINT TAB(X1,Y1);"  ";
1010  Y1=Y:X1=X
1020  I$=INKEY$(0)
1030  IF I$="A" THEN PROC_ROAD(7)
1040  IF I$="Z" THEN PROC_ROAD(14)
1050  X=X+1:IF X > 18 THEN X=2
1060  Y=Y-INT(2*RND(1)):IF Y < 0 THEN Y=19
1070  GO=GO+1:IF GO < 50 THEN GOTO 950
1080  ENDPROC
1090  DEFPROC_ROAD(L)
1100  COLOUR WH:PRINT TAB(0,L);CA$;"-----------------"
1110  FOR D=1 TO 100:NEXT D
1120  PRINT TAB(0,L);CA$;"                 "
1130  IF Y=L THEN EN=1
1140  ENDPROC
```

ELEMENTARY STATISTICS

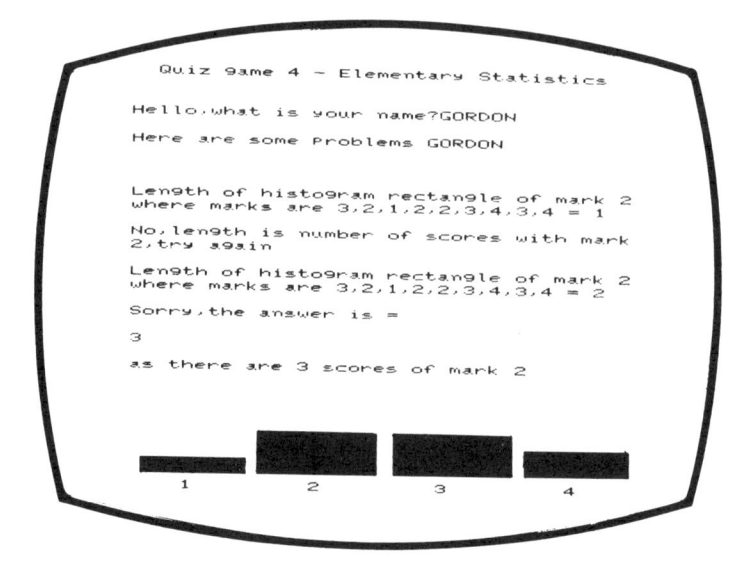

```
     Quiz game 4 - Elementary Statistics
 Hello, what is your name?GORDON
 Here are some problems GORDON

 Length of histogram rectangle of mark 2
 where marks are 3,2,1,2,2,3,4,3,4 = 1
 No, length is number of scores with mark
 2, try again
 Length of histogram rectangle of mark 2
 where marks are 3,2,1,2,2,3,4,3,4 = 2
 Sorry, the answer is =
 3
 as there are 3 scores of mark 2


   ▂▂▂  ▄▄▄▄  ▄▄▄▄  ▄▄▄▄
    1     2     3     4
```

Could you draw a bar chart (histogram) of a given set of numbers?

Could you understand a bar chart which someone else had written? Here you can test your knowledge on bar charts and means by answering as many questions on these subjects as possible, in five minutes.

This program has an added feature which is that the bar chart will be drawn, by the computer, at the end of the problem. In addition an explanation will be provided.

How to play

You will be given five minutes to answer as many questions as possible, and you may press P and RETURN for pass if you cannot work out an answer.

You will not be penalised for 'passes'.

At the end of five minutes, or sooner if you enter N for NO in answer to the question "do you want any more", your score sheet showing tries, correct answers and average time per answer will appear. If you wish to proceed then press Y and RETURN and the program will continue to ask you questions.

You can have two tries at each question if you wish. After the first attempt you will be given a hint as to the correct answer. If your second answer is wrong you will be told the solution and how it was obtained.

If you cannot work out an answer then press ? and RETURN and your computer will turn into a calculator and you can then use the normal mathematical symbols on the keyboard. To clear the calculator from the screen press AC and RETURN. For the calculator's answer press = and RETURN. To return to the main game press ? and RETURN. Always remember to press RETURN after each required response.

Programming hints

The box chart is drawn using solid squares. These are user defined characters with all the pixels filled in and are created at the beginning of the program using VDU 2 3. The bar chart is held in N(0) and N(1). The number of each of the marks are held in the array F and the bar chart is drawn from this.

You could increase the number of scores. To do this you must increase the maximum value of J in line 310. The array D would have to be reDIMensioned in line 30. Remember also, if more scores are used then the sum or the marks must be divided by a number larger than 9 in line 430 to get the correct mean value.

The maximum number of any particular mark would also be greater than 9 so the maximum value of I in line 510 would have to be increased.

```
     10    REM QUIZ            - ELEMENTARY STAT
ISTICS
     20    REM COPYRIGHT (C) G.LUDINSKI 1983
     30    DIM F(4),D(9),N$(1),IP$(255)
     40    MODE 4
     42    VDU 23,224,255,255,255,255,255,25
5,255,255
     50    S$="
                "
     52    HC$=" Highest score ":HK$="        S
core "
     60    COLOUR 1:COLOUR 128:PRINT:PRINT:P
RINT:PRINT:PRINT"    Quiz game 4 - Element
ary Statistics"
     70    PRINT:PRINT
     80    INPUT"Hello,what is your name",NA
M$:PRINT:PRINT"Here are some problems ",
:IFNAM$ <> "NO SOUND" THENPRINTNAM$ELSEP
RINT
     90    W=1:C=0:T=1:I$="":TIME=0:P=0:MAX=
0
     100   P=P+1
     110   PROC_QUESTION
     120   PRINT:PRINT
     130   PRINT:PRINTQ$" = ",:PROC_KEYIN:PR
INT
     140   IFI$="?"THEN PROC_CALC
     142   IF A=0 AND I$ <> "0" THEN GOTO 19
0
     150   IF ABS(VAL(I$)-A)<= X AND I$<>""
THEN GOTO 170
     160   GOTO 190
     170   PRINT:PRINT"Yes,congratulations":
C=C+1:PRINT:IFNAM$="NO SOUND"THENGOTO220
     180   SOUND1,-10,12,10:SOUND1,-10,20,10
:SOUND1,-10,28,10:SOUND1,-10,32,20:SOUND
1,-10,14,20:GOTO220
     190   IF T=1 THEN PRINT:PRINT"No, "H$",t
ry again":T=2:GOTO 130
     200   PRINT:PRINT"Sorry,the answer is =
":PRINT:PRINT L$:PRINT:PRINT M$
     210   PRINT:PRINTN$(1);N$(0)
     220   IF TIME >= 30000 THEN PROC_SCORE
     230   PRINT:PRINT"Do you want more ? (Y
/N)",:PROC_KEYIN:PRINT
     240   IF I$<>"Y" AND I$<>"N" AND I$<>""
```

```
              AND I$<>"YES" AND I$<>"NO" THEN GOTO 23
0
   250   IF I$="Y" OR I$="YES" OR I$="" TH
EN T=1:CLS:GOTO 100
   251   PROC_SCORE:GOTO 9999
   252   DEFPROC_QUESTION
   260   L$="":M$="":N$(0)="":N$(1)="":S=0:
F(1)=0:F(2)=0:F(3)=0:F(4)=0:G$="":FOR J=
1 TO 9
   270       D(J)=RND(4):G$=G$+STR$(D(J))+",
 ":S=S+D(J)
   280       FOR K=1 TO 4:IF D(J)=K THEN F(K
)=F(K)+1
   290         NEXT:NEXT:W=-W:G$=LEFT$(G$,17
)
   300   Z$=" where marks are "+G$
   310   IF W=1 THEN X=0
   320   IF (S/9)=INT(S/9) THEN GOTO 380
   330   INC=9*INT(S/9)+9-S
   340   D(9)=D(9)+INC
   350   G$=LEFT$(G$,16)+STR$(D(9))
   360   S=S+INC
   370   Q$="Mean mark scored where marks a
re "+G$
   380   H$="mean = total marks scored / n
umber ofscores":A=INT(S/9)
   390   L$=STR$(A)+" as sum of ("+G$+")/9
 = "+STR$(A)
   400   IF W=1 THEN M$="":GOTO 510
   410   X=0:P$=STR$(RND(4)):A=F(VAL(P$))
   420   Q$="Length of histogram rectangle
 of mark "+P$+Z$
   430   H$="length is number of scores wi
th mark "+P$
   440   L$=STR$(A):M$="as there are "+STR
$(A)+" scores of mark "+P$:IF A=1 THEN M
$="as there is 1 score of mark "+P$
   450   N$(0)="":N$(1)=""
   460   FOR I=9 TO 1 STEP -1:FOR K=1 TO 4
   470     IF F(K)>=I THEN N$(INT(I/5))=
N$(INT(I/5))+" "+STRING$(9,CHR$(224))
   480     IF F(K)<I THEN N$(INT(I/5))=N
$(INT(I/5))+"          "
   490       NEXT K:NEXT I
   500   N$(0)=N$(0)+"     1          2
    3          4"
   510   ENDPROC
   520   DEFPROC_CALC
   530     VP=VPOS:PRINT TAB(0,22);"
Calculator mode                "; TAB(0,22
)
   540   B$=""
   550   I$=GET$:PRINTI$;:B$=B$+I$:IFI$ <>
"=" ANDI$ <> "?" ANDB$<>"AC" THENGOTO550
   560   IFB$="?"ORI$="?" THENGOTO600
   570   IFB$="AC" THENPRINTTAB(0,23);S$;TA
B(0,22):B$="":GOTO540
   580   IFLEN(B$)<=1 THENGOTO540
   590   PRINTEVAL LEFT$(B$,LEN(B$)-1);TAB
(0,22):GOTO540
   600   PRINTTAB(0,22);S$;S$;TAB(0,VP-1):
PROC_KEYIN:PRINT
   610   ENDPROC
   612   DEFPROC_KEYIN
   620   IX=1:VP=VPOS:HP=POS
   630   IP$(IX)=INKEY$(10):IF IP$(IX)=""
THEN COLOUR 0:COLOUR 129:PRINT TAB(0,1);
INT(TIME/100);"      ";HC$;MAX;HK$;C:COLOU
R 1:COLOUR 128:GOTO 630
```

```
640    PRINT TAB(IX+HP,VP);IP$(IX);:IX=I
X+1:IP$(IX)=GET$:IF IP$(IX) <> CHR$(13)
THEN GOTO 640
650      I$="":FOR I=1 TO IX-1:I$=I$+IP$(
I):NEXTI
660    ENDPROC
670    DEFPROC_SCORE
680    CLS
690    PRINT:PRINT
700    PRINT:PRINT"Number of Problems co
mpleted = ";P
710    PRINT:PRINT"Number correct = ";C
720    TM=INT(TIME/100):PRINT:PRINT"Time
 taken in seconds = ";TM
730     IF C <> 0 THEN PRINT:PRINT"Time
per Problem = ";INT(TM/C)
740    IF C > MAX THEN MAX=C
750    TIME=0:P=0:C=0
760    ENDPROC
9999   REM
```

3D BRAINSTORM

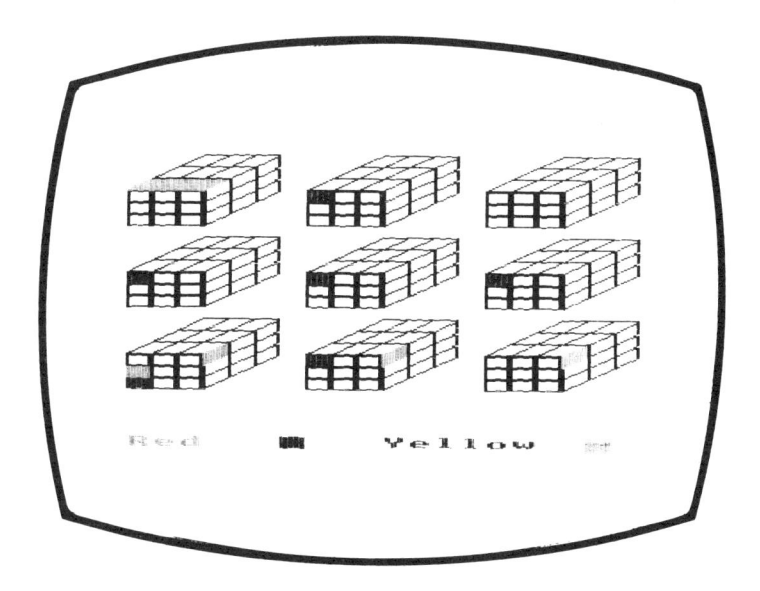

If you feel like some brainstorming, how about this three-dimensional game for two players. It is like three-dimensional noughts and crosses, except it has the advantage that all faces can be seen at a glance.

Nine cubes are displayed on the screen and each face of each cube is divided into nine squares. Your aim is to colour in a row or column of squares of any face of a cube, or to have a row or column of cubes in which you have coloured in the same square. For example, in the screen shown above, the red player has coloured in a row of squares on the top left hand cube. Also the yellow player has coloured in all the top left-hand squares on the faces on the front of the central cubes, so he has both a row and column of squares coloured in.

How to play

Players should take turns to colour in a square. The first player will colour in red, and the second in yellow. Squares are coloured in by moving the cursor (flashing underline symbol) to point to the correct square using the arrow keys.

If the square is on the front or top face or a cube, it is pointed to by putting the cursor under the square. If it is on the side of a cube it is pointed to by putting the cursor in the centre of the square. When the correct square has been selected, the space bar must be pressed and the appropriate square will be coloured in.

The score is shown at the bottom of the screen. The colour of the square between the titles indicates whose turn it is to play.

If you complete a row or column the computer makes an arcade-like warbling sound. If you try to colour in a square that does not exist a low constant note sounds.

Programming notes

The logic for a game like this is more complicated than you would expect because of the number of possible moves. The program is made more comprehensible and the program length reduced by using functions. These functions however, do not deal with numbers but with logical operators. For example, in line 160 FNX will be true if XX is less than 0 or greater than 20. This is a check that regularly has to be done to see if the X-coordinate of the object would fit on the screen.

You could make this into a one player game by allowing the computer to make random guesses. You would do this by putting IF T = -1 THEN in front of line 520. You may also add the extra line IF T = 1 THEN PS = RND(21)-1 : VP = RND(24)

```
   10   REM 3D BRAINSTORM
   20   REM COPYRIGHT (C) G.LUDINSKI 1983
   30   MODE 5
   40   DIM L%(20,24),M%(20,24),SC(2),R(6
,2)
   50   REM
   60   REM LOGICAL FUNCTIONS
   70   REM
   80   DEF FNL1(I)=(PS=0+I OR PS=1+I OR
PS=2+I OR PS=7+I OR PS=8+I OR PS=9+I OR
PS=14+I OR PS=15+I OR PS=16+I)
   90   DEF FNL2(I)=(VP=7+I OR VP=8+I OR
VP=9+I OR VP=14+I OR VP=15+I OR VP=16+I
 OR VP=21+I OR VP=22+I OR VP=23+I)
  100   DEF FNL7(P,I)=(P=I OR P=I+7 OR P=
I+14)
  110   DEF FNLP(I,J)=(IF PS=I AND VP=J)
  120   DEF FNF=(FNL1(0) AND FNL2(0))
  130   DEF FNT=((FNL1(0) AND (VP=6 OR VP
=13 OR VP=20)) OR (FNL1(1) AND (VP=5 OR
VP=12 OR VP=19)) OR (FNL1(2) AND (VP=4 O
R VP=11 OR VP=18)))
  140   DEF FNE=(FNL7(PS,6) ORFNL7(VP,10)
 OR(FNL7(PS,0) AND(FNL7(VP,4)   ORFNL7(V
P,5))) OR(FNL7(PS,1) ANDFNL7(VP,4)) OR (
PS < 0 OR PS > 20 OR VP< 4 OR VP >24))
  150   DEF FNE2=(((FNL7(PS,3) OR FNL7(PS
,4) OR FNL7(PS,5)) AND FNL7(VP,9)) OR ((
FNL7(PS,4) OR FNL7(PS,5)) AND FNL7(VP,8)
) OR (FNL7(PS,5) ANDFNL7(VP,7)))
  160   DEF FNX(XX)=(XX < 0 OR XX > 20)
  170   DEF FNY(YY)=(YY < 4 OR YY > 24)
  180   DATA 1,2,1,-1,-1,-2,7,14,7,-7,-7,
-14
  190   FOR I=1 TO 6:READ R(I,1):READ R(I
,2):NEXT
  200   REM
  210   REM SHAPE DEFINITIONS
  220   REM
  230   VDU 23,224,&01,&02,&04,&08,&10,&2
0,&40,&FF:REM /_
  240   VDU 23,225,&01,&02,&04,&08,&10,&2
0,&40,&80:REM /
  250   VDU 23,226,&FF,0,0,0,0,0,0,0:REM
_
  260   VDU 23,227,&81,&82,&84,&88,&90,&A
0,&C0,&80:REM 1/
  270   VDU 23,228,&80,&80,&80,&80,&80,&8
0,&80,&80
  280   VDU 23,229,&FF,&81,&81,&81,&81,&8
1,&81,&FF:REM LI
  290   VDU 23,230,&01,&03,&05,&09,&11,&2
1,&41,&81:REM /1
  300   VDU 23,231,&82,&83,&85,&89,&91,&A
1,&C1,&81:REM 1/1
  310   VDU 23,232,&FF,&FE,&FC,&F8,&F0,&E
0,&C0,&80:REM TOP DIAG
  320   VDU 23,233,&01,&03,&07,&0F,&1F,&3
F,&7F,&FF:REM LOWER DIAG
  330   VDU 23,234,&FF,&FF,&FF,&FF,&FF,&F
F,&FF,&FF:REM FILLED IN
```

```
 340    L$=CHR$(224):D$=CHR$(225):T$=CHR$
(226):V$=CHR$(227):U$=CHR$(228):S$=CHR$(
229)
 350    DU$=CHR$(230):VU$=CHR$(231):D1$=C
HR$(232):D2$=CHR$(233):F$=CHR$(234)
 360    FOR J=4 TO 24:FOR I=0 TO 20:L%(I,
J)=0:M%(I,J)=0:NEXT:NEXT
 370    BL=0:RD=1:YE=2:WH=3:B=128
 380    REM
 390    REM DRAW CUBES
 400    REM
 410    COLOUR BL+B:COLOUR WH:CLS
 420    FOR Y0=3 TO 17 STEP 7
 430      FOR X0=0 TO 14 STEP 7
 440        PROC_CUBE(X0,Y0)
 450      NEXT X0
 460    NEXT Y0
 470    VDU 30
 480    T=1:SC(0)=0:SC(2)=0
 490    REM
 500    REM MAIN CYCLE
 510    REM
 520    I$=GET$:PS=POS:VP=VPOS
 530    IF FNE OR FNE2 THEN SOUND1,-15,50
,10:GOTO 520
 540    IF ABS(M%(PS,VP))=1 THEN SOUND1,-
15,50,10:GOTO 520
 550    T=-T:IF T=-1 THEN COLOUR RD ELSE
COLOUR YE
 560    IF FNF THEN PROC_PUT(PS,VP,F$):GO
TO 590
 570    IF FNT THEN PROC_PUT(PS,VP,D2$):P
ROC_PUT(PS+1,VP,D1$):GOTO 590
 580    PROC_PUT(PS,VP,D2$):PROC_PUT(PS,V
P+1,D1$)
 590    M%(PS,VP)=T:VDU 30
 600    PROC_TEST:COLOUR 1+(-T+1)/2:PRINT
 TAB(6,28);F$
 610    COLOUR RD:PRINT TAB(0,28);"Red";:
COLOUR YE:PRINT TAB(10,28);"Yellow"
 620    COLOUR RD:PRINT TAB(0,30);SC(0);:
COLOUR YE:PRINT TAB(10,30);SC(2)
 630    GOTO 520
 640    REM
 650    DEFPROC_CUBE(X0,Y0)
 660    PRINT TAB(X0,Y0);"  ___"
 670    PRINT TAB(X0,Y0+1);"  ";L$;L$;L$;
DU$
 680    PRINT TAB(X0,Y0+2);" ";L$;L$;L$;D
$;VU$
 690    PRINT TAB(X0,Y0+3);L$;L$;L$;D$;V$
;VU$
 700    PRINT TAB(X0,Y0+4);S$;S$;S$;V$;V$
;V$
 710    PRINT TAB(X0,Y0+5);S$;S$;S$;V$;V$
 720    PRINT TAB(X0,Y0+6);S$;S$;S$;V$;
 730    ENDPROC
 740    DEFPROC_PUT(PX,PY,C$)
 750    IF L%(PX,PY)=0 THEN COLOUR B+BL E
LSE COLOUR B+1+(L%(PX,PY)+1)/2
 760    PRINT TAB(PX,PY);C$;
 770    IF L%(PX,PY)=0 THEN L%(PX,PY)=T
 780    COLOUR B+BL
 790    ENDPROC
 800    DEFPROC_TEST
 810    FOR J=4 TO 6
 820      PROC_CHECKX:PROC_CHECKY
```

```
 830     NEXT J
 840   IF NOT FNF THEN GOTO 880
 850   FOR J=1 TO 3
 860     PROC_CHECKX:PROC_CHECKY
 870     NEXT J
 880   IF NOT FNT THEN GOTO 930
 890   FOR J=1 TO 3
 900     PROC_CHECKXY
 910     PROC_CHECKX
 920     NEXT J
 930   IF FNF OR FNT OR FNE OR FNE2 THEN GOTO 980
 940   FOR J=1 TO 3
 950     PROC_CHECKXY
 960     PROC_CHECKY
 970     NEXT J
 980   ENDPROC
 990   DEFPROC_CHECKX
1000   IF FNX(PS+R(J,1)) OR FNX(PS+R(J,2)) THEN GOTO 1020
1010   IF M%(PS+R(J,1),VP)=M%(PS+R(J,2),VP) AND M%(PS+R(J,2),VP)=T THEN SC(T+1)=SC(T+1)+1:PROC_SOUND
1020   ENDPROC
1030   DEFPROC_CHECKY
1040   IF FNY(VP+R(J,1)) OR FNY(VP+R(J,2)) THEN GOTO 1060
1050   IF M%(PS,VP+R(J,1))=M%(PS,VP+R(J,2)) AND M%(PS,VP+R(J,2))=T THEN SC(T+1)=SC(T+1)+1:PROC_SOUND
1060   ENDPROC
1070   DEFPROC_CHECKXY
1080   IF FNX(PS+R(J,1)) OR FNY(VP-R(J,1)) OR FNX(PS+R(J,2)) OR FNY(VP-R(J,2)) THEN GOTO 1100
1090   IF M%(PS+R(J,1),VP-R(J,1))=M%(PS+R(J,2),VP-R(J,2)) AND M%(PS+R(J,2),VP-R(J,2))=T THEN SC(T+1)=SC(T+1)+1:PROC_SOUND
1100   ENDPROC
1110   DEFPROC_SOUND
1120   ENVELOPE 1,1,-26,-36,-45,255,255,255,127,0,0,-127,126,0
1130   SOUND 1,1,100,50
1140   ENDPROC
```

BAR CHARTER

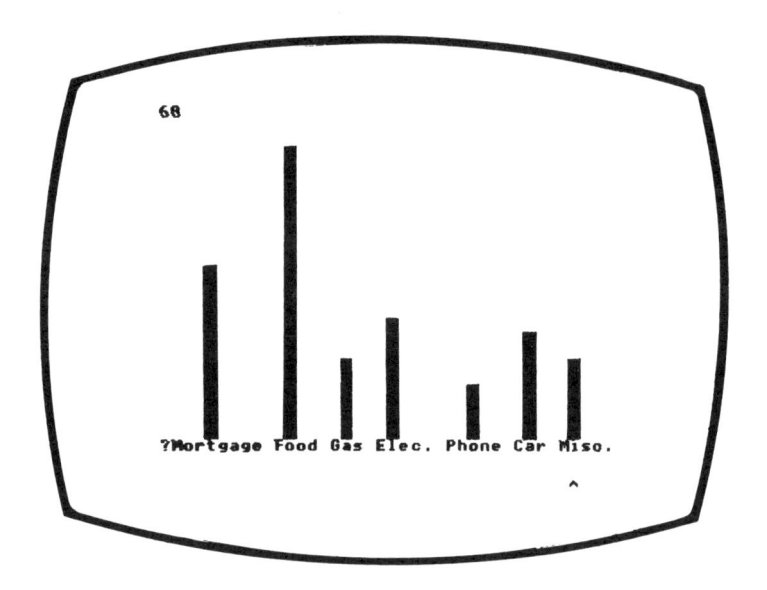

This is a versatile program that will enable you to record your expenses, club accounts or any collections you have. You could also use the printouts to impress the boss. It is easy to use and allows a maximum of 40 bars to be drawn of any height. As you key in data you watch the bar chart grow. After you have done this, you have an option of printing out the bar chart on your printer. After this the height of each is displayed.

How to use it

First you are asked for the labels of the bars in the bar chart. There may be any number but all the labels must fit on one display line. When you have keyed in a line of labels press RETURN once. Then you use the left and right ARROW keys to move a pointer at the bottom of the screen. When the pointer (symbol ∧ is positioned under the label you wish to point to, press the space bar and the bar above that label will increase in height. Each time you press the space bar, the number at the top left hand side of the screen increases by one.

If a bar gets so high that it would go off the screen, then the entire bar chart moves downwards so you are looking at the top half of the bar chart.

If you want to print out the bar chart onto a printer, if you have one, press P. The procedure PROC_DUMP supplied is for printing, using the BBC recommended printer, the Seikosha printer. If you have another one, then replace this with the appropriate screen dump routine. Your dealer, computer magazine or the maker should be able to help you.

If you want to miss out the print out and go straight to the next stage, press S. This section prints out the total for each item of the bar chart.

Programming hints

The program incorporates a scroll downwards. If you list a program, you will notice that if the program has more than around 30 lines the screen scrolls upwards. The screen can be made to scroll downwards by displaying something on the top screen line and then executing VDU 11 (cursor up). Everything on the screen will now move down one screen line.

This program has been written in MODE 4 because it requires a 40 column screen and yet it must run on a BBC Model A computer, as well as the Model B and Electron. However, MODE 4 only displays two colours. If more colours are required and you have a Model B BBC Micro or an Electron, then you may change it to MODE 1. This will allow red and yellow to be used as well. The COLOUR 129 on line 380 is now red, and can be changed to COLOUR 130 for yellow, or COLOUR 131 for white, to allow red and yellow bars to be displayed as well. The easiest way would be to display bars in different colours, depending upon where on the screen they are displayed. The variable X is the column position of the bar.

```
 10    REM BAR CHARTER
 20    REM COPYRIGHT (C) G.LUDINSKI 1983
 30    MODE 4
 40    DIM Y(40)
 50    VDU 19,0,4,0,0,0
 60    COLOUR 128:COLOUR 3
 70    CLS
 80    LA$=CHR$(136):RA$=CHR$(137)
 90    REM
100    REM INPUT LABELS
110    REM
120    PRINT TAB(10,26);"What are the labels"
130    INPUT L$:IF L$="" THEN VDU 11:GOTO 130
140    IF LEN(L$) > 40 THEN VDU11:VDU 11:PRINT TAB(0,28);STRING$(40," ");:VDU11:VDU 11:GOTO 130
150    PRINT TAB(0,26);STRING$(40," ");
160    S=0:X=1:FOR I=1 TO 40:Y(I)=26:NEXT I
170    *FX4,1
180    SC=0:DT=0
190    REM
200    REM KEY IN DATA
210    REM
220    REPEAT S=S+1
230    I$=GET$:IF I$ <> LA$ AND I$ <> RA$ AND I$ <> "S" AND I$ <> " " AND I$ <> "P" AND I$ <> "p" THEN GOTO 230
240    IF (I$=LA$ AND X=1) OR (I$=RA$ AND X=40) THEN GOTO 230
250    IF I$=" " THEN DT=DT+1:PRINT TAB(0,2);DT
260    IF I$=LA$ THEN X=X-1
270    IF I$=RA$ THEN X=X+1
280    PRINT TAB(0,30);STRING$(39," ");:PRINT TAB(X,30);"^";
290    REM
300    REM SCROLL DOWN IF CHART GOES TOO HIGH
310    REM
320    IF Y(X)+SC >=0 THEN GOTO 370
330    COLOUR 0:COLOUR 128:PRINT TAB(0,0);"S";:VDU 11:PRINT TAB(0,3);" ";TAB(0,27);STRING$(199," ");:COLOUR 1:PRINT TAB(0,2);DT;TAB(0,28);L$;:SC=SC+1
340    REM
350    REM ADD MORE TO BAR
360    REM
```

```
370     IF I$ <> " " THEN GOTO 410
380     COLOUR 0:COLOUR 129
390     YT=Y(X)+SC:IF YT > 26 THEN YT=26
400     PRINT TAB(X,YT);" ";:Y(X)=Y(X)-1:COLOUR 1:COLOUR 128
410     UNTIL I$="S" OR I$="s" OR I$="P" OR I$="p"
420     IF I$="P" OR I$="p" THEN PROC_DUMP
430     REM
440     REM TOTALS
450     REM
460     CLS
470     PRINT TAB(17,1);"Totals":PRINT TAB(17,2);"_____":PRINT
480     FOR I=1 TO 40
490       PRINT MID$(L$,I,1);" ";:IF 26-Y(I)<> 0 THEN PRINT 26-Y(I);
500       PRINT
510       IF I=26 THEN PRINT:PRINT "Press Return to continue";:INPUT RB$:CLS:PRINT:PRINT
520     NEXT I
530     *FX4,0
540     GOTO 700
550     DEFPROC_DUMP
560     VDU 2,1,8
570     FOR Y=1023 TO 0 STEP -28
580       FOR X=0 TO 1279 STEP 4
590         CH=1
600         FOR D=27 TO 0 STEP -4
610           CH=CH*2
620           IF POINT(X,Y-D) > 0 THEN CH=CH+1
630         NEXT
640         VDU 1,CH
650       NEXT
660       VDU 1,10
670     NEXT
680     VDU 1,15,3
690     ENDPROC
700     END
```

STATS PAINTER

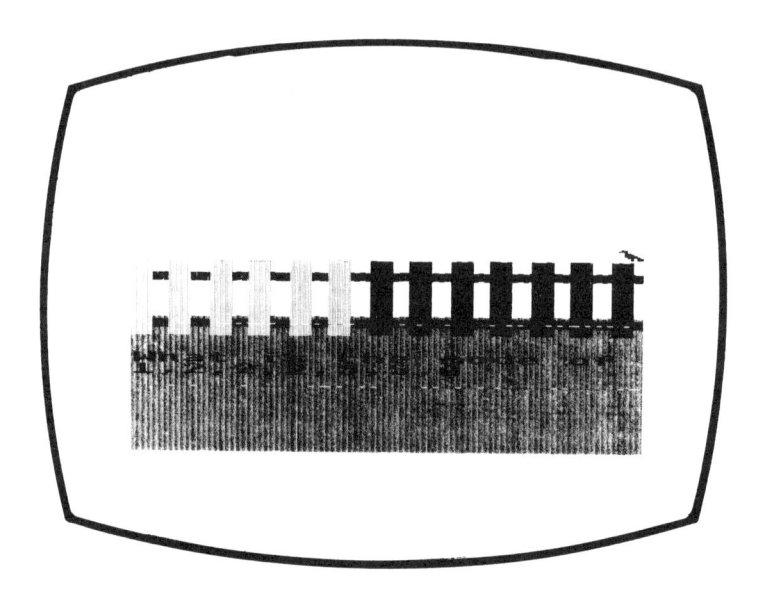

You are the director of Rockets Unlimited, and yesterday you were very pleased in the way the company was going. Then these officious accountants came, studied the figures and reckoned you were making a loss.

All weekend the sales figures are preying on your mind. Even while you are painting the fence you are trying to find out where the accountants went wrong. Sometimes you get so lost in thought that you end up painting the bird on the fence. If you do, it chirps in disapproval. If you can work accurately and quickly, you will find out where the accountants went wrong, and you will be able to prove to them that Rockets Unlimited is the success you always knew it was.

How to play

The questions are on the modes or medians of a given set of numbers. The mode of a set of numbers is the number occurring most frequently. The median of a set of numbers is the middle number. The numbers are arranged in ascending order. Just key in the answer without pressing RETURN.

If you are right you may move on to the next question by pressing RETURN. If you are wrong, or take too long to answer, the bird ends up by getting painted. After nine consecutive correct answers you find out where the accountants went wrong.

Programming hints

You can make the program easier by allowing more time to answer each question. To do this increase the 30 in line 370.

If you wish to use the graphics but to set different types of questions, replace procedures PROC_STAT, PROC MODE and PROC_MEDIAN. Assign the question to Q$, the answer to A$ and the hint to H$. Questions in this program must have answers one digit or letter long. This could be changed, though, by changing the input routine at line 370.

```
 10    REM STATS PAINTER
 20    REM COPYRIGHT (C) G.LUDINSKI 1983
 30    MODE 5
 40    DIM D(15),C(5)
 50    CLS
 60    VDU 19,0,4,0,0,0,19,2,2,0,0,0
 70    GOTO 200
 80    REM
 90    REM U.D.G. CALCULATOR
100    REM
110    DEF FNB(N$)
120    TF=0
130    FOR L=0 TO 7
140        TF=TF+(2^L)*VAL(MID$(N$,8-L,1))
```

```
150     NEXT L
160   =TF
170   REM
180   REM BIRD SHAPE
190   REM
200   VDU 23,224,FNB("01100000"),FNB("1
1100000"),FNB("00110000"),FNB("00111000"
),FNB("00111100"),FNB("00011110"),FNB("0
0001011"),FNB("00001011")
210   REM
220   REM DRAW FENCE
230   REM
240   FOR J=1 TO 9
250     COLOUR 128:CLS
260     GCOL 0,2:PROC_BLOCK(0,0,1280,45
0)
270     GCOL 0,3
280     FOR I=0   TO 1240 STEP 100
290       PROC_BLOCK(I,400,50,200)
300     NEXT I
310     PROC_BLOCK(0,420,1280,20):PROC_
BLOCK(0,550,1280,20)
320     COLOUR 3:COLOUR 128:PRINT TAB(1
9,12);CHR$(224)
330     COLOUR 3:COLOUR 130
340     PROC_STAT
350     PRINT TAB(0,21);Q$
360     GCOL 0,1:I=-100:I$="":ID=0
370     I$=INKEY$(30):IF I$="" OR ID=
1 THEN I=I+100:PROC_BLOCK(I,400,50,200):
IF I < 1140 THEN GOTO 370
380     IF I$=A$ AND ID=0 THEN PRINT:PR
INT:PRINT"Yes,you are right":GOTO 420
390     IF I < 1000 THEN PRINT I$;:ID=1
:GOTO 370
400     COLOUR 1:COLOUR 128:PRINT TAB(1
9,12);CHR$(224):FORII=1 TO 3:SOUND1,-15,
250,4:SOUND1,0,0,1:SOUND1,-15,250,4:SOUN
D1,0,0,2:NEXT:COLOUR 3:COLOUR 130
410     PRINT TAB(0,26);"No,";H$
420     COLOUR 3:PRINT TAB(0,30);"Hit R
eturn for more";:INPUT RB$
430     IF I$ <> A$ THEN GOTO 250
440   NEXT J
450   PRINT TAB(0,27);"Eureka! you fou
nd  it.Get on the phone quick
    ":GOTO 810
460   REM
470   DEFPROC_BLOCK(X,Y,W,H)
480   MOVE X,Y:MOVE X+W,Y
490   PLOT 85,X,Y+H
500   PLOT 85,X+W,Y+H
510   ENDPROC
520   DEFPROC_STAT
530   MC=0:DN=1:MO=0:W=RND(2)
540   FOR I=1 TO 5
550     C(I)=INT(RND(1)*4):IF C(I)=MC T
HEN GOTO 550
560     IF C(I) > MC THEN MC=C(I):MO=I
570     IF C(I)=0 THEN GOTO 620
580     FOR JJ=DN TO DN+C(I)-1
590       D(JJ)=I
600     NEXT JJ
610     DN=DN+C(I)
620   NEXT I
630   IF DN/2=INT(DN/2) THEN DN=DN+1:D(
DN)=6
640   D$="":FOR I=1 TO DN:D$=D$+STR$(D(
I))+",":NEXT:D$=LEFT$(D$,(DN*2)-1)
```

```
650    TH$="th":MM=INT(DN/2)+1:IF MM=1 T
HEN TH$="st"
660    IF MM=2 THEN TH$="nd"
670    IF MM=3 THEN TH$="rd"
680    IF W=1 THEN PROC_MODE
690    IF W=2 THEN PROC_MEDIAN
700    ENDPROC
710    DEFPROC_MODE
720    Q$="What is the mode of "+D$
730    A=MO:A$=STR$(MO)
740    H$="there are more "+A$+"s"
750    ENDPROC
760    DEFPROC_MEDIAN
770    Q$="What is the median  of "+D$
780    A=D(1+INT(DN/2)):A$=STR$(A)
790    H$=A$+" is middle no."
800    ENDPROC
810    END
```

WHO DUNNIT

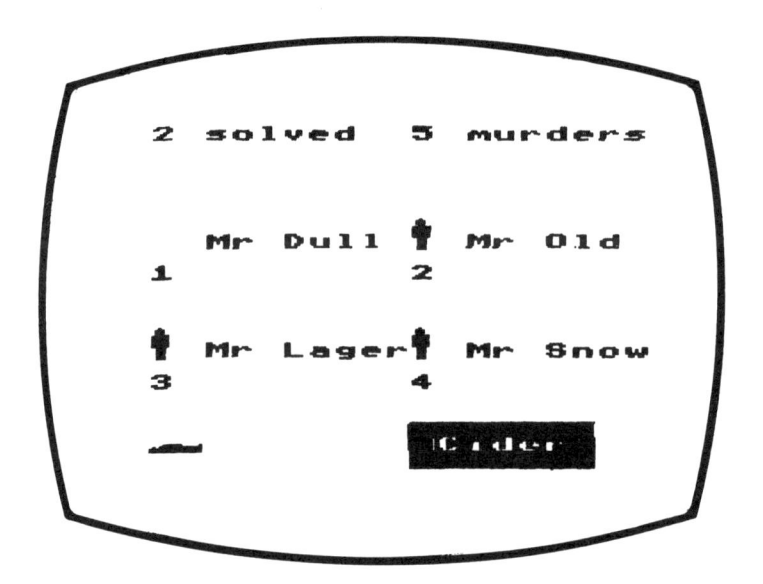

```
2 solved   5 murders

   Mr Dull ♀ Mr Old
 1         2

♀ Mr Lager♀ Mr Snow
 3         4

  ▬          Order
```

Looking through the window you see him standing in his study. Then you hear a gun shot and he falls to the ground. You walk into the house and go into his study.

There are four men there. You know their names. You find a note which he must have written before he died. This is a clue to the murderer. You must decide which of the four men is the murderer before they slip out the room.

How to play

The victim's note is by the man lying down. You must work out which of the names of the other men has some connection with this word. For example, in the screen show above, Mr Lager is the murderer as Lager and Cider are both drinks. Alternatively words that are related may have the same or opposite meanings. For example, Big and Large, also Hot and Cold are related.

Key in the number below the suspected murderer, (3 in this case) before the four men disappear off the screen.

If you are right, you hear police sirens as the police cars approach. If you are wrong or too late, you do not. The score is given on the top line. Press RETURN to play again.

Programming hints

This program illustrates how the ENVELOPE statement can be used to create sound effects. This allows the pitch or the amplitude (volume) of a note to be continuously varied in a short time or both. As a gun shot has a constant pitch the three pitch parameters of the ENVELOPE statement in line 410 are zero. As a gun shot has a sharp attack phase and a slower delay the volume initially shoots up to maximum 126 before going down more slowly. This is the 126 after the 10. ENVELOPE statements are quite complicated but you can find the ENVELOPE statement you require with limited knowledge by trial and error.

If you want to add more words to the game, add some more DATA statements at the end of the program. Put in sets of three words that are related. Read the other words in lines 740 and 760 for ideas. Make sure that each set is not related to the other words in those lines. When you have added the extra words, count up the total number of sets of words from line 740 and assign it to TT in line 310.

```
10    REM WHODUNNIT
20    REM COPYRIGHT (C) G.LUDINSKI 1983
30    MODE 5
40    DIM WD$(30,3),N(5),X(4),Y(4),P1$(
2),P2$(2)
50    X(1)=0:Y(1)=7:X(2)=10:Y(2)=7:X(3)
=0:Y(3)=14:X(4)=10:Y(4)=14
60    SC=0:TU=0
70    GOTO 200
80    REM
90    REM U.D.G. CALCULATOR
100   REM
110   DEF FNB(N$)
120     TF=0
130     FOR L=0 TO 7
140       TF=TF+(2^L)*VAL(MID$(N$,8-L,1))
150     NEXT L
160   =TF
170   REM
180   REM SHAPES OF MEN
190   REM
200   BD=FNB("01111100"):LG=FNB("001110
00")
210   VDU 23,224,FNB("00010000"),FNB("0
0111000"),FNB("00111000"),FNB("00010000"
),BD,BD,BD,BD
220   VDU 23,225,BD,BD,LG,LG,LG,LG,LG,L
G
230   VDU 23,226,0,0,0,0,FNB("00001111"
),FNB("01011111"),255,255
240   VDU 23,227,0,0,0,0,FNB("11000001"
),255,255,255
250   M$=CHR$(224)+CHR$(10)+CHR$(8)+CHR
$(225):V$=CHR$(226)+CHR$(227)
260   B=128:BL=0:RD=1:YE=2:WH=3
270   COLOUR B+BL:COLOUR WH
280   REM
290   REM READ WORDS
300   REM
310   TT=25
320   FOR II=1 TO TT
330     READ WD$(II,1),WD$(II,2),WD$(II
,3)
340   NEXT II
350   TIME=0
360   REM
370   REM UPRIGHT MAN AND GUN SHOT
380   REM
390   CLS:COLOUR B+BL:COLOUR WH:PRINT T
AB(0,20);M$
400   *FX15,0
410   ENVELOPE1,1,0,0,0,100,20,10,126,
-50,-1,-76,126,126:SOUND0,1,6,255
420   FOR I=1 TO 4
430     N(I)=RND(TT)
440   NEXT I
450   IF N(1)=N(2) OR N(1)=N(3) OR N(1)
=N(4) OR N(2)=N(3) OR N(2)=N(4) OR N(3)=
N(4) THEN GOTO 390
460   REM
470   REM DRAW PEOPLE AND NAMES
480   REM
490   TU=TU+1
500   SN=RND(4)
510   FOR I=1 TO 2
520     P1$(I)=WD$(N((2*I)-1),RND(3)):P
2$(I)=WD$(N(2*I),RND(3))
530     COLOUR WH:PRINT TAB(0,7*I);M$;:
COLOUR YE:PRINT " Mr ";P1$(I);:COLOUR WH
```

```
       :PRINT TAB(10,7*I);M$;:COLOUR YE:PRINT "
    Mr ";P2$(I)
    540      PRINT TAB(0,(7*I)+3);2*I-1;TAB(
10,(7*I)+3);2*I
    550      NEXT I
    560      VC$=WD$(N(SN),RND(3)):IF VC$=P1$(
1) OR VC$=P2$(1) OR VC$=P1$(2) OR VC$=P2
$(2) THEN GOTO 560
    570      MU$=" "+VC$+" "
    580      PRINT TAB(0,20);" "
    590      COLOUR WH:PRINT TAB(0,21);V$;:COL
OUR B+WH:COLOUR WH:PRINT TAB(10,20);MU$;
:COLOUR RD:PRINT TAB(10,21);MU$;:COLOUR
WH:PRINT TAB(10,22);MU$:COLOUR B+BL
    600      K=1
    610      I$=INKEY$(100):IF I$="" AND K < 5
    THEN PRINT TAB(X(K),Y(K));" ";TAB(X(K),
Y(K)+1);" ":K=K+1:GOTO 610
    620      REM
    630      REM POLICE SIREN
    640      REM
    650      IF VAL(I$)=SN THEN FOR K=1 TO 4:S
OUND 1,-15,109,10:SOUND 1,-15,101,10:NEX
T:SC=SC+1
    660      REM
    670      REM SCORE
    680      REM
    690      COLOUR WH:PRINT TAB(0,1);SC;" sol
ved";TAB(10,1);TU;:IF TU > 1 THEN PRINT
" murders" ELSE PRINT " murder "
    700      COLOUR WH:PRINT TAB(0,28);"Press
Return":INPUT RB$:GOTO 390
    710      REM
    720      REM DATA
    730      REM
    740      DATA Big,Small,Large,Fat,Thin,Plu
mp,Quiet,Loud,Noisy,Wet,Dry,Damp
    750      DATA Hot,Cold,Warm,A,Z,Alpha,Good
,Bad,Nice,Mad,Crazy,Sane,Dull,Shiny,Matt
,See,Hear,Feel,Old,Young,Aged,Laugh,Cry,
Weep,Kid,Child,Adult,Am,Pm,Noon,Bird,Fow
l,Beast,Snow,Ice,Sleet,Beer,Lager,Cider
    760      DATA King,Queen,Jack,Give,Take,Gr
asp,BBC,ITV,Ch. 4,Ill,Well,Sick,Gym,PT,P
E,Red,Amber,Green,Load,Save,Chain,Eye,I,
Aye
```

WORD SEARCH

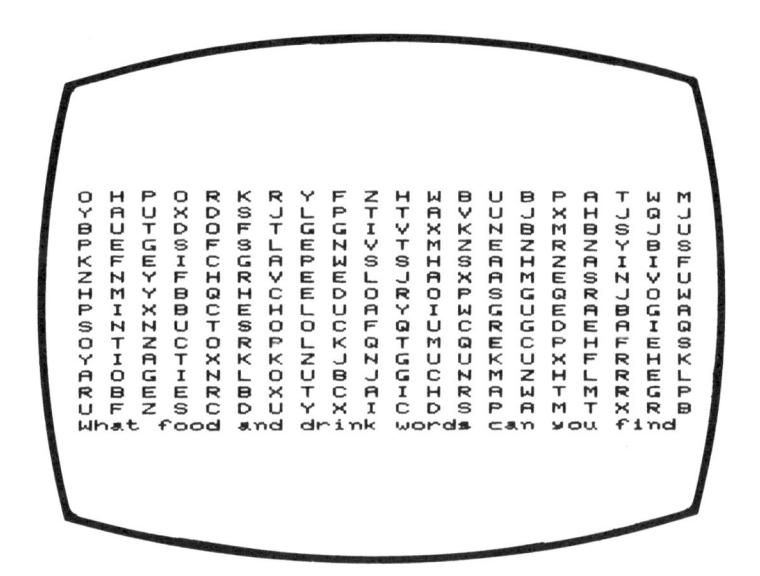

```
O H P O R K R Y F Z H W B U B P A T W M
Y A U X D S J L P T T A V U J X H J Q J
B U T D O F T G G I V X K N B M B S J U
P E G S F S L E N V T M Z E Z R Z Y B S
K F E I C G A P W S S H S A H Z A I I F
Z N Y F H R V E E L J A X A M E S N V U
H M Y B Q H C E D O R O P S G Q R J O W
P I X B C E H L U A Y I W G U E A B G A
S N N U T S O O C F Q U C R G D E A I Q
O T Z C O R P L K Q T M Q E C P H F E S
Y I A T X K K Z J N G U U K U X F R H K
A O G I N L O U B J G C N M M Z H L R E L
R B E E R B X T C A I H R A W T M R G P
U F Z S C D U Y X I C D S P A M T X R B
What food and drink words can you find
```

This is a brainteaser you have probably come across in puzzle magazines, but that doesn't make it any easier.

The words which are hidden in the screen spaghetti are all four letter — related to food or drink.

How to play

When you have found one of the twenty words on the screen, key it in and press RETURN.

If your guess is correct your word will be ticked, if wrong it will be crossed. Your score will be displayed to the right of the word keyed in by yourself. After five seconds the word will be erased and your next word must be entered.

The words you have found to date will be blanked out on the screen, which should make it easier for you to spot the others.

To change the screen key in NEXT and press RETURN.

Programming hints

Two methods are used to reduce the memory required in this program. First, all the numerical arrays are integer arrays, this is shown by putting a % sign after the variable names. Secondly the possible words are stored one after another in a string, instead of an array.

Another change that you could make is to alter the words that can be found. There are 57 of them in order to make the puzzles as random as possible. These words are stored in the variable W$ on line 70. If you can think of other four-letter words to do with food or drink, then just replace some of the words with those you have chosen. If you want to put in words on a different subject, then think of a subject and replace the words in W$ with your words all joined together. Remember there must be 57 of them, and they must all have four letters.

If you wish to use longer or shorter words, all words must still be of the same length as each other. Change the words in W$ so the total number of letters is still the same. Then change ID in line 240 so 4 is replaced by the number of letters in each word, and 57 is replaced by the maximum number of words in W$. The minimum value of ID must be 1 so 3 should be changed accordingly. The 4 in line 280 should also be changed. If the word length is increased more elements of array L$ must be checked to be empty and then assigned a letter in lines 290 to 310. Also the 80 (which is 20 words of 4 letters) and 4 in line 520 should be changed. The 4 in line 530, and the 3 and 4 in line 570 should also be changed.

Special feature

If you wish to have a collection of word search puzzles to be completed away from the computer, and you have a 40 column printer, then press CNTRL B then RUN the program and the puzzles will be printed out for you. Press CNTRL C after you have finished.

```
LIST0 7
>LIST
    10    REM WORD-SEARCH
    20    REM COPYRIGHT (C) G.LUDINSKI 1983
    30    MODE 4
    40    DIM L$(24,18),CH%(20,14),P%(20)
    50    VDU 23,224,0,1,2,4,8,16,160,64
    60    VDU 23,225,255,255,255,255,255,25
5,255,255
    70    W$="FISHMEATCAKESOUPPEASSALTCHOPC
ORNWINEBEERLIMEBRANBEANVEALROLLHAKEPIKER
OCKSPAMMALTROLLMINTLAMBPORKBEEFTARTCANEN
UTSTUNARICESAKISAGOLOAFGAMEHERBPEARMILKL
ARDCHIPSTEWOATSPATESAGEMACECRABMASHCOLAP
ITHPEELSOYALEEKDUCKDILLYOLKBALMSUETSODA"
    80    P%(0)=240
    90    REM
   100    REM GENERATE LETTERS
   110    REM
   120    CLS
   130    WC$="":CR=0
   140    FOR I=1 TO 14
   150      FOR J=1 TO 20
   160        L$(J,I)=""
   170        CH%(J,I)=0
   180      NEXT J
   190    NEXT I
   200    FOR I=1 TO 20
   210      D=RND(3)
   220      R=RND(10):IF D=2 THEN R=RND(14)
   230      C=RND(16):IF D=1 THEN C=RND(20)
   240      ID=4*RND(57)-3
   250      FOR Q=0 TO I-1:IF ID=P%(Q) THEN
 GOTO 240
   260      NEXT Q
   270      P%(I)=ID
   280      WD$=MID$(W$,ID,4)
   290      IF D=1 AND L$(C,R)="" AND L$(C,
R+1)="" AND L$(C,R+2)="" AND L$(C,R+3)="
" THEN FOR K=0 TO 3:L$(C,R+K)=MID$(WD$,K
+1,1):CH%(C,R+K)=I:NEXT K:GOTO 330
   300      IF D=2 AND L$(C,R)="" AND L$(C+
1,R)="" AND L$(C+2,R)="" AND L$(C+3,R)="
" THEN FOR K=0 TO 3:L$(C+K,R)=MID$(WD$,K
+1,1):CH%(C+K,R)=I:NEXT K:GOTO 330
   310      IF D=3 AND L$(C,R)="" AND L$(C+
1,R+1)="" AND L$(C+2,R+2)="" AND L$(C+3,
R+3)="" THEN FOR K=0 TO 3:L$(C+K,R+K)=MI
D$(WD$,K+1,1):CH%(C+K,R+K)=I:NEXT K:GOTO
 330
   320      GOTO 210
   330      WC$=WC$+WD$
   340    NEXT I
   350    REM
```

```
360     REM DISPLAY LETTERS
370     REM
380     FOR I=1 TO 14
390       FOR J=1 TO 20
400         IF L$(J,I)="" THEN PRINT TAB(
2*J-2,I*2-1);CHR$(64+RND(26));" ";:GOTO
420
410         PRINT TAB(2*J-2,I*2-1);L$(J,I
);" ";
420       NEXT J
430     NEXT I
440   REM
450   REM CHECK ANSWER
460   REM
470   FOR N=1 TO 20
480     PRINT TAB(0,29);"What food and
drink words can you find              ";
490     VDU 11
500     INPUT I$
510     IF I$="NEXT" THEN GOTO 120
520     FOR M=1 TO 80 STEP 4
530       IF I$ <> MID$(WC$,M,4) THEN
GOTO 610
540       PRINT TAB(8,30);CHR$(224);:CR
=CR+1:PRINT TAB(35,30);CR;
550       FOR I=1 TO 14
560         FOR J=1 TO 20
570           IF CH%(J,I)=(M+3)/4 THEN
PRINT TAB(2*J-2,I*2-1);CHR$(225);
580         NEXT J
590       NEXT I
600       GOTO 630
610     NEXT M
620     PRINT TAB(8,30);"  X";:RB$=INKE
Y$(500):GOTO 480
630   NEXT N
```

The author of this book specialises in the marketing of educational software.

Full details and prices can be obtained by sending a S.A.E. to:

> **G. Ludinski,
> 26 Avondale Avenue,
> Staines,
> Middlesex.**